No Way Out
Keys to Avoiding Suicide

Dr Carla Cornelius

Jesus Joy Publishing

Published and printed in Great Britain in 2016 by Jesus Joy Publishing.

ISBN 978-1-90797-145-7

Jesus Joy Publishing
is a division of Eklegein Ltd
www.jesusjoypublishing.co.uk
20161010

Dedication

This book is for those who experience suicidal thinking and tendencies.

To those who wrestle with this subject because of their families, friends or professions, thank you for not burying your heads in the sand as so many do. May you always find more cause to be hopeful than to despair.

To those individuals and organisations working tirelessly to stem the tide of this human tragedy each life saved makes all your efforts worthwhile.

Also, to all those who have succumbed to suicide. They are too numerous to mention but their lives speak volumes as do their deaths.

About the Book

The premise of this book is that a change of heart can emerge, through empathy and the right questions, without the need for outside intervention. It promotes avoidance rather than prevention because the former empowers individuals to change their minds and lives for the better; the latter requires awareness of suicide intention by a third party which is not always possible. It is based on the premise that ultimately you can save your own life with a change of heart and discovery of purpose. The world does not need to read another obituary but it does need to hear your story of survival.

This book is not just a textbook but a workbook. Therefore, to get the most out of it, the reader is encouraged to answer the questions in the space provided where it is marked *"your response"*. The responses are for your sole benefit, but writing them will help you to organise and clarify your thoughts.

About the Author

Carla Cornelius, Ph.D. gained her doctorate from Trinity School of the Bible and Theological Seminary in Newburgh, Indiana. Her dissertation proposed a biblical model of counselling the suicidal based on the book of Ecclesiastes.

She currently resides in Staffordshire, England with her husband, Michael, with whom she partners in business and ministry. She is an accredited Methodist preacher and pastoral counsellor.

Acknowledgements

To my husband, Michael, for bearing with me and lending his professional input as this book metamorphosed into its final state. You are a remarkable embodiment of perseverance and going the extra mile.

To my son, Fela, who daily inspires me to keep living.

To my parents, Richard and Hazel, who have made a tremendous investment in me since conception, and who demonstrate by example that life is truly worth living at all stages and seasons.

Contents

Part 4

Foreword

"When you get stranded, the way to start moving again is not to search for an answer but to find a new question to which your life can be the answer."[1]

You have probably forgotten just how amazing you are. It's no wonder you have been fighting an internal battle – a silent conflict which no one has seen and none may be aware of. You may find it almost impossible to share your pain because you think it will not make any difference. You look around you, and earthly life may seem like a continual round of struggles until you draw your last breath.

It is possible to teach hopeless people like yourself to think in a hopeful way. This not just an exercise in positive thinking; as I will attempt to show you, there is good reason to be hopeful. This book will contain some thought-provoking questions – they are not meant to overwhelm you but shake you out of your current pattern of thinking. It might

1   Rabbi Jennifer E. Krause.

be helpful to take some time to think about the answers and make some notes if you would find that helpful. Take as long as you need.

The human struggle comes in many shapes and forms. Who could not help but be amazed by the five personalities featured in the TV series 'My 600Ibs Life'.[1] Trapped inside morbidly obese bodies they had indulged with food and which had betrayed them, they finally found a surgeon brave and compassionate enough to do gastric bypass surgery in order for them to have even the tiniest chance of survival. Cameras tracked their journeys over the course of seven years where they battled weight loss and gain, ill health and near death experiences, as well as private and public humiliation. Harsh and scornful words were often hurled in their direction, but as one of them said, there was nothing anybody said which came close to being as bad as what they said to themselves on a daily basis. I could well imagine the fear and self-loathing they experienced in their heads, words such as:

"I'm no good."

---

1 http://www.tlc.com/tv-shows/my-600-lb-life/

"I'll never amount to anything."

"I'm ugly/disgusting/hideous."

"My life is worthless."

Psychological pain has the potential to be more disabling than physical pain. Very often it's caused by the words which echo in our minds - the criticisms of others or our own self-critique - which cause us the most distress.

Q: So, what are you saying to yourself on a regular basis?

[your response]

As strange as it sounds, you might not be aware of how negative your thinking has become, and how it is shaping your decisions and behaviour.

We all have problems but if you think you are the

problem, then it might seem logical to think that eliminating yourself will be the solution. You will never know whether your death really solved the problem because you would no longer be around to make that evaluation.

> **Q:** Are you really seeking to solve the problem or do you simply want to end your pain, whether physical or emotional?

[your response]

As two researchers have pointed out - *"suicide does not make pain go away. It simply transfers the pain to everyone left behind..."*[1] - someone closely connected to you and who cares about you. Yes, it may surprise you that there are those who care

---

1   Dr Darcy Haag Granello and Dr Paul F. Granello, *"Identifying Suicidal Signs"*, http://factbasedhealth.com/identifying-suicidal-signs/; accessed December 11, 2015.

about you even if you do not care about yourself. Your death would negatively impact on someone, even someone you may never have met.

You are more than a statistic. Your death would be a significant loss to humanity as you are unique with a special blend of gifts, personality traits and acts of service to render. Your family and friends would never recover from such a trauma. Husbands and wives would be filled with guilt, wondering whether they could have done anything more to prevent such an outcome; parents will wonder if they contributed through some parenting deficiency to your becoming such a lost soul; your children will wonder if they are doomed to share your fate. In all cases, a lifetime of wondering about the life you could have lived, would be theirs.

With every death by such means there is a deepening fault line in the human landscape, and the extent of the repercussions may not be witnessed until many years later. A suicide can simply never be forgotten. In terms of immediate impact, it can have a ricochet effect of copycat suicides. It is a brutal blow to the psyche of surviving humanity;

it's not just the families or close friends who may be deemed suicide survivors - we are all suicide survivors! Let us survive together.

Part 1 The Reasons

"The bend in the road is not the end of the road unless you refuse to take the turn."

Anonymous

Chapter 1

Trauma

What would motivate you to make the final plunge towards self-destruction? With you, as with many others, there might be a complex web of reasons - not just one.

Paul Tautges, author of 'Counselling One Another' recognises that other factors besides mental illness can trigger suicidal feelings, citing examples such as *"anger, revenge, remorse and drug and alcohol abuse."*[1]

In a way, we all have the potential to commit suicide, but what most of us are able to brush aside and overcome, others may find so overwhelming that the only reasonable course of action appears to be self-destruction. The eventual trigger may simply be the straw which breaks the camel's back. Dr. Donald Scott in his book 'Coping with Suicide', explains that it may be preceded by several disastrous events occurring within a short

---

1   Paul Tautges, *"11 Myths and Misperceptions about Suicide,"* counselingoneanother.com, (accessed August 15, 2013).

space of time.[1]

Q: Has this been the case with you?

[your response]

It may seem brave to soldier on after a trauma, but suppression of trauma can mean that your sadness, anger and pain build up and eventually reach a tipping point when suicide seems the only way out.

It is possible for a singular trauma to predispose someone to suicide for the remainder of his or her mortal life. This may have been the case with Isabelle Blow whose brother died by accident whilst she was supposed to be watching him. Though only five at the time, she may have carried inside her an unspoken sense of guilt for the rest of her life until

1   Donald Scott, Coping with Suicide (Overcoming common problems), (London: Sheldon Press, 1989), 38.

her tragic death by suicide at the age of 48. Her means of death – self-poisoning with weedkiller - would suggest an inner compulsion to punish herself. Perhaps she wanted to feel pain before she died, as she most invariably would have. Perhaps she reasoned sub-consciously that her deceased brother had suffered pain whilst he was dying and therefore so should she, not to mention the lifetime of grief experienced by her parents which would no doubt have exacerbated her sense of guilt.

Those in certain professions face trauma on an almost daily basis. Examples are police officers, doctors and nurses, soldiers and war veterans. BLUE[1] is a documentary which addresses the occupational hazards and gives a riveting insight into the pressurised daily life of a police officer in the 24th and 25th police districts of Philadelphia, USA. Those who witness death everyday and who may feel responsible for causing the death of others, either by acts they have done or failed to have done, are particularly susceptible to thoughts of suicide and attempts. Not only have they been de-sensitised to death, but they are expected to be

---

1   http://vimeo.com/105656376; BLUE app - https://itunes. apple.com/us/app/the-blue-app/id931490733?mt=8&ign-mpt=uo%3D4.

strong and have strong coping mechanisms. They live with this belief system and fear admitting that they are not coping in case they lose the respect of their peers or their jobs.

Q: In what ways can you identify with these professionals?

[your response]

We all, to some extent, live in our own worlds with our feelings locked away safely within us. We all have an image we present to the world by accident or design to which we and they have grown accustomed and which people have come to expect. But sometimes some of the things we try to hide, end up killing us. Perhaps, there is a positive way for you to alleviate your frustrations or anxieties – a way that works for you.

In the UK, suicide is the most common cause of death among men between the ages of 15-44?[1] If you are male, it might help you to feel less of an oddity to know that other men also struggle to open up and admit they are struggling. In such situations where suicide occurs, the shock and grief experienced by survivors, are heightened because it appears so senseless.

A case in point was the suicide of Gary Speed, MBE. This Wales football manager stunned his circle of friends and acquaintances, and indeed the wider world. He seemed to have so much to live for – glittering career, wife, children. Hours before he took his life by hanging, he had been interviewed for TV and appeared jolly and in good spirits.

The truth may yet unravel, but this tragedy points to a tendency common to all humanity – the fact that we wear masks. Indeed, in the words of the Prophet Jeremiah, *"the heart is deceitful above all things... Who can know it?"*[2] It may be difficult for you to understand fully what's driving your death

1 www.mind.org.uk, accessed 4/02/2008; ONS, 2003, Health Statistics Quarterly, trends in the mortality of young adults aged 44 in England and Wales, 1961-2001, available: www.statistics.gov.uk/pdfdir/hsq0803.pdf.

2 Jeremiah 17:9.

wish. So often we don't understand why we feel the way we do.

It doesn't matter how popular you are, how many friends you have, how big the crowd in which you find yourself, the fact remains that we are all essentially individuals who live in our own private worlds. Only we decide who will gain access, or whether anyone at all.

We remain so fearful of sharing our own thoughts; experience may have taught us that others will only dismiss or belittle them. Yet, we were made for sharing. So much of artistic expression – painting, literature, drama and music – stems from the need to give expression to something which, if left inside, will only overwhelm us.

Such people do not necessarily cry for help because they have become skilled at concealment. There is a simultaneous sense of sub-conscious shame that, were their secret to be revealed, those closest to them would feel let down - even betrayed. Hence, the suicide is a way out of this dilemma, and away of safe-guarding the loved one from this disappointment.

Some people manage to war a mask so well that they lead parallel lives; the pretend life begins to take precedence over the real life; or they begin to become blurred such that they do not know what's real and what isn't.

Q: Are you leading a double life? Are you contemplating suicide as a way to end your confusion?

[your response]

Wanting to kill yourself is not a weakness, it is a human instinct in times of great pressure, psychological or physical pain, or sense of purposelessness and despair. The authors of the 'Comprehensive Textbook of Suicidology' have observed that - *"Individuals who are in pain, hopeless, depressed, anxious, psychotic, have a right to relief short of irreversible cessation of their consciousness (i.e. death)."*[1] Pain can be relieved to a degree with anti-depressants; it can be denied through a lifestyle of avoidance. Rather than seek to suppress your pain as an inconvenient truth, have you considered that it is a sign that something is wrong which needs to be addressed?

Those who are plagued by the death wish may be in a state of anticipatory grief. By playing and re-playing their deaths in their minds, they begin to mourn the loss as if it has already happened. Why not consider sharing your thoughts with someone you trust as a way of breaking the cycle of negative thinking.

---

1   Ronald W. Maris et al., Comprehensive Textbook of Suicidology (New York: Guildford Press, 2000),.6. Reprinted with permission of The Guildford Press

Chapter 2

Overwhelming Grief

You may regard life as no longer worth living because of the absence of a loved one through death, divorce or abandonment. But bereavement is not limited to the death of another human being, but could be as a result of any type of meaningful loss such as a pet, job, or bodily function resulting from a brain injury or lost body part such as by amputation.

Q: Are you coping with a recent loss?

[your response]

We cannot however underestimate the trauma of human loss under tragic circumstances such as through illness, crime, accident or war to mention a few. The survivors are left with the heart-wrenching sense that their loved ones' lives were needlessly cut short. What seems even more callous is how life in the wider world seems to continue on as normal as though nothing significant has occurred. It is perfectly understandable that at this juncture, survivors might not want to live any longer without their loved ones in such a cold and indifferent world. The following words were shared by one survivor under the heading 'My Beautiful Daughter' - *"I remember thinking at that time how hard it was to understand why someone who was so treasured and loved by us all decided that she was such an ugly, horrendous person that she needed to die."*[1] Such were the words of a mother who lost her daughter to suicide.

It is important to acknowledge each bereavement and recognise it as the significant trauma it is, and grieve our losses on at a time so that they do not accumulate and become overwhelming.[2]

Our lives may be so interwoven with another's that

1   Quote taken from 'Survivors of Bereavement by Suicide' with permission; www.uk-sobs.org.uk

2   Elizabeth Kübler-Ross and David Kessler, On Grief and Grieving: finding the Meaning of Grief through the Five Stages of Loss(Simon and Shuster:London, 2005), p.172.

should that person leave for whatever reason, life loses all sense of meaning. Yet the answer is not in self-destruction but a growing awareness that our lives are not inextricably bound to another human being but only and ultimately to God. Despite the heartache, you can live on without them whilst being that He holds, watches over and protects your loved one's soul, though you cannot.

As difficult as it may be, we must not be afraid to grieve the loss of a loved one. During the process, it may sometimes seem that the future is unimaginable without this person. That feeling is a testimony to how close you were. To be human is to feel; to feel deeply is when we are most human. The stronger the bond, the deeper the pain will be. But to shut ourselves off from feeling any pain in relationships, would be to shield ourselves from love, and thereby lose out on an important part of our humanity.

Chapter 3

Dying to be heard

You may feel as if your feelings and opinions do not really matter to anyone. Sadly, we have become too addicted to screens in our modern age. As such, it seems that we increasingly prefer to do relationships from behind the safety of a screen. We have forgotten the deep human need we all have to be physically touched, to make eye contact with others and to be listened to with full attention.

A 16-year old posed a question on Facebook before she took her life – *"If I were to die, would anyone cry?"* Her precipitous act of suicide meant that she did not live to hear the answer to that question – a resounding 'Yes'! No doubt, there are still tears being shed for her tragic death.[1]

At the root of many suicidal thoughts lies anger but it is a paralysing anger. Attempters and completers have convinced themselves that their circumstances or they themselves cannot be fixed.

Do you realise that your anger need not be self-

---

1   Kimberley Ripley, *"Amber Cornwell: Facebook Question Before Suicide"*, December 29, 2014, topix.com.

destructive? You can use it to improve your life or the lives of others. Many social campaigners, activists and philanthropists are motivated by anger over some injustice.

Q: Are you angry because you have been denied something which you feel is vital for your well-being?

[your response]

You might be able to relate to some or all of the following thought patterns:

'Life has not given me what I deserve, and so because life has not played fair with me, I will turn my back on it'.

'I will do as I please with my own life, and not let life's vagaries control me'.

'This will show them. They will finally realise how much they hurt me'.

If you are thinking along the lines of the third example above and you want to punish someone who has disappointed you, you need to recognise that through such drastic action, you will never have the chance to be at the receiving end of this person's change of heart. Yes, you might not have realised it but, by your intentions, it is clear this person matters to you or you would not go to such lengths to get his or her attention.

The suicide note of Nancy Motes was a case in point. She allegedly wrote:

"My mother and so-called 'siblings' get nothing except the memory that they are the ones that drove me into the deepest depression I have ever been in."

This family will never experience the reconciliation which may have freed Nancy from her depression.

You might be demoralised that life has not turned out the way you expected, that a celebrated few seem to get all the glory and affirmation while your presence and efforts go largely unnoticed whether from your family, colleagues, boss or even an industry in which you have tried to make your mark.

It is also possible that you might be angry with yourself. You might think that your loved ones and the world in general are better off without you because of your mistakes or inadequacies. Remember that you are not alone; we all have failings and inadequacies. Yet, in spite of them, you still have a lot to offer your family, community and network of friends and acquaintances.

Chapter 4

The Voice of Conscience

If you know you are responsible for the injury or death of another, there may be such a strong sense of self-condemnation that your guilt may seem too much to bear. You may be considering ending your life because you can no longer bear your own guilt and the disapproval of society.

Your action may result from a desire to avoid:

Punishment.

A confession of guilt.

Social stigma and alienation.

By doing so, you are avoiding the very thing which could bring healing to yourself and those you wronged.

We are all guilty of wrongdoing. Before God who is perfect and holy, we all stand condemned and, were it not for the grace of God, we would all be justifiably worthy of death. Because God is pure, what we consider the 'smallest' of sins is offensive to Him just as a pure white canvas is forever tarnished by even the tiniest particle of dirt. Very often we cannot see our sins for what they are because we think they are too tiny to be noticed or to have any consequence.

However, God sees the canvass of our hearts as through a microscopic lens, and each time we sin, the stain on the canvass gets bigger and bigger. Mercifully, although *"the wages of sin is death ..."*, the other side of the coin is that *"... the gift of God is life in Jesus Christ our Lord."*[1]

Jesus Christ is the only effective stain remover! He was willing to have all humanity's wrongs and misdeeds imputed to him, and to bear the punishment of death to have them expiated. But the story of God's grace did not end there - God resurrected Jesus from the grave and he now sits at the right hand of God and intercedes for all those who are willing to entrust the care of their souls to him.

We live in a society where certain acts of wrong-doing are castigated more than others; some cause the hairs on peoples' skin to stand to attention whilst others barely raise an eyebrow. If you read a list of

---

1   Romans 6:23.

'bad behaviours' in Galatians 5:19-21, you would probably think that those acts mentioned were no big deal because there are, on the whole, what we would regard as 'harmless', 'everyday' foibles such as jealousies, envy and drunkenness. Yet, we are clearly told that *"those who practise such things will not inherit the kingdom of God."* In our post-modern, western societies, the influence of moral relativity has meant that acts of wrong-doing which were once regarded as unacceptable, are now deemed to be within the parameters of individual choice. We have fudged the line between good and evil.

Yet, when we commit wrongdoing, it is not enough to dismiss it as petty or to pretend it never happened, because our consciences (that part of us we often wish we didn't have but which God designed to be the spiritual alarm bells when we are going astray), will keep reminding us that we have overstepped the boundaries.

A secret service agent recently killed himself amidst an investigation into his extramarital affair.[1] It would be all too easy to point fingers, and say

---

1   Josh Feldman, *"Secret Service Agent Commits Suicide amidst investigation into affair,"* http://www.mediaite.com/online/secret-service-agent-commits-suicide-amidst-investigation-into-affair/, accessed September 5, 2016.

that he should have thought about the implications of what he was doing before he did it. But, if all those who experience a compromised conscience, decided to end their lives, there would hardly be anyone left on the earth. There is always scope for forgiveness, redemption and another chance if we are sincere in our desire to repent, and do our best to make amends.

Although Jesus has paved the way for forgiveness, we have our part to play. We must take responsibility for our wrong-doing and acknowledge it. This not only ushers us into the spiritual presence of God and makes His grace available to us, but it facilitates the healing of those whom you may have hurt. They need to know that the person who caused them such harm is aware of the harm they have caused. Without this confession, they may carry the bitterness of the injustice or a sense of having deserved the act.

There is another side to this equation which is the scourge of shame felt by those who have been abused or victimised. They may fall prey to the misconceptions that it was their fault, they deserved it, and that God did not stop it, indeed no-one stopped it because they were worthless and not worth the effort.

It has been said that harbouring unforgiveness is like drinking poison and expecting the other person (the offending party) to die. We often fail to see how we do ourselves grievous harm (physically, emotionally and spiritually) when we refuse to forgive. Often the bitterness causes chronic or life-limiting illnesses such as ulcers or cancer. We forfeit peace of mind and inner harmony, and even God's forgiveness because the Lord's prayer reminds us that God forgives us only when we have forgiven others - *"for if you forgive men their trespasses, your heavenly Father will also forgive you: but if you do not forgive men their trespasses, neither will your Father forgive your trespasses."*[1]

The aggrieved party might protest on the basis that the wrong that has been done is just too terrible, but the sins of mankind resulted in the most terrible act of all to secure our redemption – God himself, in the person of His only Son, came to die on our behalf. Yet many do not even acknowledge God or humble themselves enough to seek His forgiveness for their sins.

1   Matthew 6:14-15

In similar fashion, those who have been wronged rarely hear any words of acknowledgement or apology from their wrongdoers. The recent suicide of a 58 year old man who had suffered years of abuse by Catholic priests when he was a youth, is a case in point[1]. We are left to wonder if he had been able to talk about his pain and distress with a compassionate third party or receive some type of counselling to work through his pain and depression. It is often the case that wounds sustained in childhood leave the deepest scars, and often take the longest to heal. But as a Chinese philosopher once said, *"the journey of a thousand miles begins with a single step"*[2]. Being willing to embark on this journey could mean the difference between life and death.

---

1   IOL, *"Widow sues Church over abuse suicide,"* http://www.iol.co.za/news/world/widow-sues-church-over-abuse-suicide-1.1416207, accessed September 5, 2016

2   Lao-tzu (604-531 BC)

Chapter 5

Rejection

You may live with a deep sense of rejection or that you don't belong to anyone or don't fit in anywhere. We are all rejected by someone at some time in our lives but sometimes the feeling lingers. Sometimes we suffer repeat rejections which only serves to deepen the scars of unworthiness.

Q: When last did you feel rejected? How did you react?

[your response]

A 'misfit' may be described as someone who is socially awkward, uncommonly shy and ill at ease in his or her own skin and society.

The misfit feels himself or herself to be at odds

with society. There is nothing wrong with feeling odd – everyone is odd in some way. Just because you are odd, doesn't mean you don't have a right to live. Whatever is different about you may be used to be of service to others in some way. Your search to find your unique calling may be taking longer than expected, but it may surprise you to know that, everyone is searching for something even those whom the media portrays as having 'arrived' or having life all figured out.

There's something unique which you have to offer which your wider circle of family, friends and acquaintances needs to see, hear and experience. If you fail to live up to this potential, they and society at large will miss out on your unique gifts. Ultimately, what matters most is not becoming well-known for your particular talents but the cumulative effect of one-to-one personal interactions.

You may have spent your whole life so far seeking to live up to what you feel is expected of you, and despite the popularity, wealth, status, applause, respect or approval you may have gained, deep down you feel a failure. It may seem too hard to leave behind what you have, to go in search of that elusive factor that is missing in your life. But that is ultimately what your life is about – to seek and find what will make you whole.

The alternative path is on display all around us – a combination of coping strategies – various forms of addiction such as to work, sex, entertainment – anything to distract ourselves from the awareness of that gaping hole inside us. Similarly, your suicidal thinking might be a coping mechanism – the promise of an escape hatch in case the 'going gets too tough'.

Each life is unique, and individuals can only discover their purpose through the inner promptings of the heart. The heart is where our dreams are incubated. We live in a modern world with advertising and stereotyping where people are encouraged to be carbon copies of one another, rather than seek to discover and pursue their own life's mission.

You may have become convinced that your life is not worthwhile because right now your life appears meaningless, when the reality is simply that you have not yet discovered the meaning of your own life. You may have become caught up in a cycle of actions and activities which others have told you will bring meaning, only to end up feeling empty and unsatisfied.

To follow your life's purpose may sometimes require that you disengage from familiar people and activities, at least for long enough for you to hear your Creator speak to you. However, the quest is never so futile that you need to disengage from life itself.

An elderly British woman who was neither terminally ill nor disabled, was recently granted a request for physician-assisted suicide at the Dignitas clinic in Switzerland. It was reported that her reasons were a sense of alienation from the modern world on the basis that *"at my age, I feel I can't adapt, because the new age is not an age that I grew up to understand. I see everything as cutting corners. All the old fashioned ways of doing things have gone."*[1] Clearly, the psychological pain she felt at not being able to adjust to the norms of modern living, was immense. But ultimately, she may have

---

1

Carrie Dedrick, *"Elderly woman granted assisted suicide after becoming disillusioned with life"*, ChristianHeadlines.com, accessed April 7, 2014.

felt too overwhelmed and isolated in her struggle to adjust. She may have felt the world had rejected her so she ended up rejecting the world.

Chapter 6

The Bitter Taste of Failure

Your worth must become in your own mind a settled, indisputable fact. Let's face it - we live in a materialistic culture which assesses people's value in terms of what they are 'worth' (their earning capacity, potential or actual income). We can so easily fall into the trap of thinking that our value is dependent on what we do. For example, rich lists correlate the top earners with their income. The term 'self-made' is a misnomer because no-one is really so; it discounts the contributions made by so many countless others who helped to shape and inspire us in ways we may not truly appreciate.

This attitude of self-reliance contradicts the inescapable truth that we did not will ourselves into existence – some force totally outside our limited understanding (Higher Power), decided we should be born – a miracle in itself considering the odds against conception. It stands to reason, therefore, that since you did not determine the act or timing of your conception and birth, you need not presume to determine the act or timing of your death. Your sole responsibility is to live to the best of your ability.

There are things in life which money can't buy and can't be valued in terms of money. According to the biblical account, Jesus poses the challenging question -*"what can a man give in exchange for his soul?"*[1] A soul, the invisible part of you which comes from God and forms your essence, is invaluable in God's eyes; you were conceived with value which does not diminish whether you are poor or rich, employed or unemployed, lower class or middle class. It is neither here nor there whether people value you since their approval is fickle and usually rooted in the thinking, whether conscious or sub-conscious of 'what's in it for me?' Jesus said *"do not worry about your life, what you will eat or what you will drink; nor about your body, what you will put on. Is not life more than food and the body more than clothing? ..."*[2]

Q: What are some of the things you are worrying about at the moment?

[your response]

1   Matthew 16:26.

2   Matthew 6:25-32.

Happiness may not be as difficult to attain as you think. Gallop's Global Wellbeing Index, ranked Panama in Central America, as the happiest place to live based on the following criteria: individual perceptions of wellbeing, social wellbeing, community wellbeing, the presence of purpose and physical health.[1] It is interesting to note that the key factor in all the criteria is individual perception.

It might amaze you to know that you possess those attributes and things which so many reckon would make their own lives complete.

Q: Has anyone ever paid you a compliment that you can remember; and if so, what was it?

[your response]

---

1 http://rt.com/news/188668-worldwide-happiness-index-wellbeing/, accessed January 18, 2015.

Perhaps you have compared your life with others and thought - 'If only…I had that education, those good looks, could afford that house, that car, had that career or spouse?' Yet those who possess these much sought-after 'assets' so often take them for granted or find that they leave them feeling empty or still wanting more.

What you value in life can determine whether you consider your life worth living or not. It is possible to live without those things which society tells us we should have, and not let it undermine our sense of self-worth.

You may have experienced an acute sense of failure or fear of simply not having what it takes. Failure can arise in any context – relationships, health, as well as work and careers. In the case of the death by suicide of Vicki Harrison, at the tender age of 21, her fatal action was clearly motivated by her sense of failure after trying for two years in vain to secure a job. On her suicide note, she wrote *"I just don't want to be me anymore."* Somewhere along the line, she had internalised the false message of the culture that 'we are what we earn or the job titles we hold.' Perhaps she thought she would always be a burden on her parents and society and had lost hope of all future prospects. It's important to remember that, as trite as it may sound, we don't fail as long as we keep trying. But what we tell ourselves in the meantime makes all the difference.

It may be tempting to want to be someone else whose life seems so much more rewarding and worthwhile compared to yours. But no one's life is as straightforward and charmed as it may appear; each individual is faced with struggles and challenges. You have the ability to change how you perceive your own challenges. It may be that you need to talk to someone who has overcome a similar challenge to gain a new perspective.

Q: Who do you know who has overcome many challenges? What can you learn from his or her example?

[your response]

Many have also embraced the myth that knowledge and education are the pathway to enlightenment and ultimate satisfaction. Consider the case of Alice McGovern – an unlikely suicide victim. She had achieved intellectual heights with four A Level grade As which had secured her a place at Oxford University. At 18 she wrote those jaw-dropping words - *"life is simply not for me"*[1], and soon after threw herself off a cliff at Beachy Head, East Sussex.

But what could Alice have known of life by the tender age of 18? Her statement begs the question – *"what is life?"* especially in light of the fact that she treated it as something which could be so hastily discarded. Jesus said that *"a man's life does not consist in the abundance of his possessions"*[2], and our certificates and the knowledge we have attained may be counted amongst our possessions.

Sometimes we think that life as we have known it so far is all there is to life. Sometimes we can be ashamed of saying that we want more out of life because this may be misinterpreted as lack

1 David Sapstead, *"'For those who loved me, please do not feel responsible…Life is simply not for me',"* The Telegraph (London, England), accessed August 5, 2005.

2 Luke 12:15.

of gratitude or ruthless ambition. What this may mean is that an individual may desire a completely different way of life. It is so sad that we can often feel trapped in our lives – the lives we have created for ourselves, not because of adverse circumstances or material hardships, but because they do not yield the satisfaction we had anticipated.

People achieve for all sorts of reasons, and for some achieving academic qualifications comes easier than for others. Honest and fulfilled living comes at the cost of sacrificing what you simply can do (we all have the potential to do so many things, and this is especially the case for those who have superior intelligence and multiple talents) to the superior pursuit of what you were born to do.

Q: What is it that inspires you, that you have secretly envisaged yourself doing for as long as you can remember?

[your response]

Your will, passion and drive may be absent from what you are doing, and you may doing it for dishonest reasons such as to meet others expectations, make money or for lack of courage to pursue what you truly desire. These may seem legitimate reasons but cannot sustain you in the long haul.

For Alice to have achieved so much academically would have required a lot of striving, coping with pressure and self-discipline. It would appear that the pay-off - public renown, peer admiration, family pride and a place at a prestigious university, was not sufficient to sustain her will to live.

This seemingly perfect, well-adjusted 'A' student who had just matriculated into a prestigious university, may have killed herself because she feels she is only living to fulfil the expectations of others. She may be afraid to voice the fact that she no longer wants to go to university and become 'the professional' she is expected to become; she may long to divert from the well-chosen plan of life set out for her, yet fear disappointing those she loves or who love her the most. Unable to reconcile the conflict within her, she may have decided that killing herself is her only option. She fails to recognise that this will be the ultimate disappointment to her loved ones, and from which there is no recovery. Sadly, she does not live to see these conflicts resolved.

Chapter 7

The Pressure to Succeed

Often the outer context or circumstances of our lives are reflected in our inner landscape and thought process. A depletion of our finances may therefore feel as if our souls and identity are also being depleted. This would explain why experts have observed that *"suicide is commonest at times of social and economic distress"*. Similarly, the Samaritans, a suicide prevention helpline, warns that suicide could rise during the economic Depression as a result of unemployment, mounting debts and house repossessions.[1] But this need not become a self-fulfilling prophecy.

Consider the case of a young woman who was a straight 'A' student and destined for the higher echelons of success.[2] She had a harmonious relationship with her boyfriend and her family, yet she killed herself. Despite the appearance of the perfect life, all was clearly not well with this

---

1   Mental Health Foundation, *"Economic Crisis Increases Suicides and Murders,"* http://www.mentalhealth.org.uk/information/news/?entryid17=73591&q=acunemploymen - accessed September 24, 2009].

2   See chapter 6.

troubled young lady. We may never know what finally pushed her over the edge. It may have been the pressure of expectation which she perceived as meaning that she could never afford to fail. The gifted often have impossibly high expectations of themselves and are tormented by their own perfectionism.

Q: Have you been asking too much of yourself? What do you think may be driving your need to be perfect?

[your response]

It may often be tempting to give up on life altogether when it does not meet with our own expectations for our lives? The benefit of maturity is that you have lived long enough to know that these expectations will often need to be adjusted at some point, but will usually be replaced by more realistic, fulfilling ones. Sometimes the greatest demand life places on us, is to endure long enough to see our lives turn out for the best despite the twists and turns along the way.

Q: What are some of the good yet unexpected things which you have experienced in your life so far?

[your response]

We forget that there is so much about life we do not choose – the time, place and family of our birth, race and nationality. We do not choose our natural talents and personality, although we may hone and develop them. If we grow up in western democracies, by the time we reach adulthood, we've been brain-washed to believe that life owes us certain basics such as a means of livelihood and a 'decent' standard of living. Therefore, by implication, if we don't have them or lose them by some misfortune, then it is tempting to conclude that life is not worth living.

Q: Do you often compare your life to others?

[your response]

Envy derives from dissatisfaction with oneself and the circumstances of one's life. It is this dissatisfaction which leads to comparison with others, and the view that one is lacking in a necessary attribute or possession. Some people hold erroneous evaluations of themselves such as believing they are unlovable or worthless.

Similarly, many believe that wealth will bring them fulfilment. In fact modern society does its best to disseminate this false value and myth. Without the means of acquiring money or the amount of money they think they need, many descend into hopelessness.

In 2009, the Director of the Department of Mental Health of the World Health Organisation forecasted that economic-motivated suicides would increase.[1] Although such warnings can alert organisations which cater to those at risk, they might also serve to fuel global panic and despair. Self-fulfilling prophecy works by convincing others or ourselves that what has been predicted must come true. It's easy to become a statistic if you feel that you have no control over your circumstances.

Jesus stated emphatically – *"A man's life does not consist in the abundance of his possessions"*[2] and *"what will it profit a man if he gains the whole world and forfeits his soul?"*[3] Although money plays a large part in the smooth functioning of society, there are traditional values of family unity, good neighbourliness, charity and community spirit

---

1   *"Warning – economic –motivated suicide will increase in 2009"*, www.aggregateresearch.com, accessed January 9, 2009.

2   Luke 12:15.

3   Matthew 16:26.

which are of more fundamental importance.

In our quest for more, it's all too easy to lose sight of these home truths. Even if we lose every penny, we still have life, and where there's life, there's hope. Tomorrow is a new day. The fact remains, no matter how much we make financially, or accumulate materially, we can't take it with us to the grave. The Old Testament character Job wisely remarked *"naked I came from my mother's womb, and naked I will return"*[1].

Regrettably, for most people it's hard to resist the lure of wealth. There are those for whom, deep down inside, there is no drive to be wealthy. Yet, they may find themselves caught up in a rat race to succeed materially for the sake of their families or significant other. The fact remains that there are enough resources in this world to meet basic human needs. For example, it is a travesty that in our modern age with international news, trade and travel, there are still many who are starving to death or going without necessary health care. Yet, the reality is that most will not be wealthy; most will live in moderate comfort but with the ever-present need to be sensible with their expenditure.

1   Job 1:21.

Most people who do not fall into the category of the wealthy, fantasize about the acquisition of wealth as a type of utopia on earth where everything goes their way, and they can have anything they want. What is often overlooked is that God made the human heart to desire things of everlasting value such as love, respect, peace and joy. The temporal acquisitions of this world, though deceptive in their appeal, can never permanently satisfy the longings of the human soul.

Nevertheless, many still harbour the misguided notion that money paves the way to happiness, and wealth guarantees you whatever your heart desires. As a consumer society, we think the more money we have, the more stuff we can buy and consequently the happier we will be. Robert W. Wilson was an 86-year-old millionaire who jumped to his death from his high-rise apartment. Even after having suffered a stroke, in theory he could have afforded the finest care in the world from the best doctors, nurses and care-givers. Wilson apparently said to a friend, that he did not want to suffer following his stroke. As a professed atheist, what was lacking in spite of all his millions, was a personal faith in God who uses what appears to be senseless human suffering for a higher and ultimate good.

His manner of death was symbolic. He seemed to have achieved the pinnacle of worldly success – what the world says should make you happy and whole - as symbolised by his acquisition of a penthouse which meant he was literally sitting on top of the world; and yet he still felt so let down by life that he chose to die.

Q: How would you personally define success?

[your response]

Success is inwardly-defined. Motivational writer and speaker, Stephen Covey, related success to mastery over yourself.[1] Onlookers may deem you as happy and successful but deep down inside you

1   Stephen Covey, The 7 Habits of Highly Effective People,(Simon and Schuster: New York, USA, 2004), 104.

may regard your life as a failure and be acutely aware that you are wearing a mask. Sooner or later, the truth will out and your life will be exposed as a sham. In Wilson's case, it was through death by his own hands. What is the point of worldly status and accolades if inside you feel miserable and a failure?

We all have a tendency to base our conclusions about another person's well-being on their outer circumstances. For those who are suicidal, life has lost its purpose or maybe they never discovered their true purpose. It is possible too that they created their own meanings which have eventually ended in futility. In today's society, this is easily done. Popular culture would have us emulate the rich and famous at the expense of our own unique identity. What peace we would derive from the decision to turn away from noise and distractions in order to listen to the voice in our hearts – the still, small voice of God.[1]

---

1   1 Kings 19:12-13.

Chapter 8

World-weariness

"I have had enough" are words which even the most world-weary amongst us would do well to avoid. When we experience a constant barrage of sameness, we may begin to project into the future based on our experience of the past. Bear in mind that throughout the course of your life, you are bound to experience many stages and seasons. Your death wish may simply be a desire for change or a wake-up call for an honest life review.

Q: What is it about myself that I no longer wish to live with?

[your response]

The principle of diminishing returns means that

what used to satisfy will no longer satisfy the longer one is exposed to it?

Some tire of the sameness of their daily lives and struggles. The French refer to this state of mind as 'ennui'. The word 'frustration' is derived from the French 'frustra' which means 'in vain'. To frustrate means 'to prevent from attaining a purpose'. Their chief frustration is that they seem unable to break the cycle of sameness. English actor, George Sanders, reportedly wrote in his suicide note -

> *"Dear World, I'm leaving you because I am bored. I feel I have lived long enough. I am leaving you with your worries in this sweet cesspool…"*[1]

Raj Persaud holds the view that *"Boredom is more profound than simply a lack of stimulation. Sometimes it is lack of any impulse at all. The problem is not finding something to do, it is finding a reason for doing anything at all."*[2] Applied Psychologists, Locke and Latham, explain that *"boredom occurs when an individual*

---

1 'George Sanders', en.wikipedia.org/wiki/ George_Sanders, accessed September 6, 2016.

2 Raj Persaud, 'Health: Today you're bored. Tomorrow you're ill…' Independent.co.uk, accessed September 6, 2016.

decides an activity has no personal significance ...they say to themselves - there is nothing in this for me... "[1]

Q: When last did you feel bored. What were you doing at the time, and what was the trigger?

[your response]

It may be that you have been engaging in activities which do not hold true meaning and purpose. Your seeming inability to change your predicament may cause you to begin to view the future as a life sentence from which death is the only escape.

We all get stuck in a rut from time to time, and this usually arises from the constant repetition of the same thing. Indeed, we tend to gravitate to something new in a quest to break the monotony

1   Locke, E.A., & Latham, G.P (1990). *A Theory of Goal Setting and Task Performance.* Upper Saddle River, N.J : Prentice Hall.

of human existence. Such a sense of monotony can lead us to question or take for granted the significance of what we do, and feel unappreciated which can in turn lead to self-pity. If this cycle is not quickly broken, we can begin to drift through life and form the opinion that we are surplus to requirements, and therefore that no-one will miss us if we're gone.

Chapter 9

Copycats & Suicide Pacts

In both these cases, the suicide is embarked on because of another suicide. In the first case of those who feel they have no option but to replicate the suicide of another person, this is usually because their love and admiration for the first suicide completer is such that they cannot envisage life without them. In other situations, it may arise from a group influence as occurs in cults or tight-knit communities where the leaders hold such sway that they are able to convince the followers to kill themselves individually or en masse, usually as a way of achieving a better after-life. Also a history of suicide in the family can raise a spectre which haunts family members who may sense an inevitable slide into similar despair.

If you are thinking of resorting to a copycat suicide or pact, consider that you are using the other person with whom you wish to make this pact, to eliminate your doubts and strengthen your resolve. However, your doubts should not be so easily dismissed but act as a powerful tool to prompt you to re-examine your situation.

Q: Are you willing to consider both sides of
the argument rather than just surround
yourself with those who think suicide is
your only option. Can you think of another
life-affirming alternative to suicide?

[your response]

For those who have resorted to this fatal course
of action, there was no doubt someone or some
case which influenced them in that direction.
For example a celebrity suicide will attract far
more media attention than the death of someone
anonymous, but this does not mean their lives
were more valuable than those who live and die in
relative obscurity.

All human life is important in some way, and only

God knows for sure why their souls were given breath and the impact they had and were meant to have.

You are your greatest work. The only life you can live fully is yours. We often live vicariously through the lives of others whose lives seem more fulfilled such as celebrities whose widespread images portray lives of glamour, adventure and indulgence. Let us remember that pictures often lie, since no-one's life is as perfect as it may appear, and that each life holds validity and value.

From January 2007 until February 2012, there were seventy-nine suicides in Bridgend in South Wales, the victims ranging from 13-41.[1] The town has quickly earned the reputation as a suicide hotspot. In the journalist's attempt to grab attention, they may be giving the wrong impression to any impressionable residents that the town is somehow cursed, and that for troubled youth who live there, they have no option but to take this fatal step.

The Werther effect is a phrase coined from the suicide of the fictional hero in the book 'The

---

1   Luke Salkeld, 'In a town shattered by a series teenage suicides, another young girl takes her own life,' Daily Mail, accessed March 20, 2008.

Sorrows of Young Werther' by Johann Wolfgang von Goethe. Its publication in 1774 triggered a spate of young male suicides.

They have told themselves time and time again that they cannot live without this person. Such an agreement between strangers is often little more than a way of summoning up the courage to go ahead with an act which they instinctively resist. Our peers can influence us to do things which we wouldn't otherwise do on our own. The fact that you are seriously considering a suicide pact suggests that you have doubts and are seeking someone else to strengthen your resolve. Because killing yourself is such an extreme decision, you ought to hear all sides of the argument rather than just surround yourself with those who share your view that killing yourself is the right solution. The danger of a pact is that you can never vouch for the honesty and resolve of the other person. Questions arise such as who will be the first to venture into the great unknown? Will the surviving person chicken out at the last minute, then by left with a lifetime of guilt and possibly legal repercussions such as a law suit for aiding and abetting the suicide of another?

Suicide pacts may be entered into by parties who are known to one another or by complete strangers. Those who are co-dependent often feel their lives are not worth living without a significant other. Most couples do not enter into suicide pacts. Most bereaved spouses do not jump into the grave besides their dearly departed. Does this mean that they love them any less than those who would resort to this option? A thousand times 'No'! When you have truly known what it is to love and be loved, you know your loved ones will want the best for you even when it means picking up the pieces of your life, and going on without them.

The questions arise:

Who will keep the memory of your loved ones alive if you follow them to the grave?

Who will continue the good work they have started and help to preserve their legacy?

Yours may be as the lone voice to attest to the fact that your loved one ever existed, and was loved and valued?

Chapter 10

Living with Unbearable Pain

The pain-ridden live in bodies which are wracked by pain with no let-up. They may be under extreme physical pressure where an agonising death seems imminent, yet sometimes they are told that their agony may be prolonged until they finally succumb. Living with no prospect of recovery may seem like an intolerable death sentence. There will be times in all our lives which seem intolerably dark and gloomy.

If you are aware that something or someone is causing you pain, try your best to distance yourself from the source. If you don't understand your pain - why you feel and act as you do - determine to spend the rest of your natural life seeking the answer. If you have been told that there is nothing you can do about your pain, recognise that this is the opinion of one or at best a few - 'experts' though they may claim to be. Determine to spend the time you have left seeking other views. Never allow yourself to be limited to one opinion, but determine to become the 'expert' of your own life.

Find out what makes you tick, what agrees with you and what brings out the best in you in terms of the things you do each day which either aggravate or palliate your pain. It will no doubt take trial and error but this is what life is all about. This is a gift that only you can give to yourself.

Q: Are you willing to begin to keep a diary for pain management? Today, what will you enter under the headings 'aggravate' and 'palliate'?

[your response]

Psychological pain can be just as debilitating as physical pain. For example, many women suffer with post-natal depression commonly thought to be due to hormonal imbalances in the aftermath of giving birth. Their anguish may be heightened by their acute awareness that their feelings are completely at odds with how they 'should' be feeling. They may also fear being labelled a 'bad mother'. According to the National Health Service in England, it affects *"more than one in ten women within a year of giving birth"*.[1]

What is deemed as bearable pain by one person, may be considered unbearable by another. We would each benefit from understanding our personal pain thresholds which refers to the amount of pain we can tolerate before life begins to become unbearable. Just as modern medicine offers analgesic medication and devices for coping with physical pain, there are coping mechanisms for dealing with psychological pain.

Pain serves the purpose of communicating to us that we are in danger of injuring ourselves, or that something in our bodies or lives is out of balance, broken or malfunctioning.

Q: When you look back at your life so far, is there anything you learned from painful experiences?

---

1   NHS Choices, 'Postnatal Depression', http://www.nhs.uk/ conditions/Postnataldepression/Pages/Introduction.aspx, accessed September 26, 2016.

[your response]

It is of tremendous benefit to seek to develop a positive outlook. With time and focus you can begin to nurture steely determinaton that whatever life throws at you can be endured and overcome. The psalmist wrote – *"I would have lost heart, unless I had believed that I would see the goodness of the Lord in the land of the living."*[1] Psychologist, Abraham Maslow, wrote *"People who have been made secure and strong in the earliest years, tend to remain secure and strong thereafter in the face of whatever threatens."* They are said to have a high tolerance for frustration. It is not so much what happens to you but whether or not you have the inner strength to cope with it. There are those who seem to get a head start on inner strength, but that does not mean that it cannot be acquired later in life.

1   Psalm 27:13.

Chapter 11

Escaping from Reality

Those who are in denial about their own mortality often appear to be living life to the full. In reality, they may be addicted to a lifestyle of thrill-seeking in the form of drug-taking, extreme sports, and promiscuity even though they put their own lives and others at risk through these high-risk lifestyles. It is often the case that those who engage in such dangerous activities are escaping from the emotional demands of their lives. Similarly, the much-respected modern tendency towards workaholism may be a socially acceptable way of avoiding confrontations at home such as a nagging spouse, overly-demanding kids or even the fact that there is no-one to come home to.

Q: Where do you go to seek refuge from harsh realities?

[your response]

We often seek refuge in things which ultimately disappoint such as drugs, entertainment, sex, shopping or relationships. Suicide is most commonly associated with substance misuse, and the most commonly used and accessible substance is alcohol.[1] Binge drinking which is defined as *"drinking lots of alcohol in a short space of time or drinking to get drunk"*[2], has also emerged as a socially acceptable way to relax, escape or avoid pain and responsibilities.

For so many, revealing their innermost fears and anxieties, does not come easy. We may have been raised in a household where 'the stiff upper lip' was considered the best way of dealing with problems. Ironically, such people can find themselves drawn to friends and life partners who embody the exact opposite and were raised to be expressive and confrontational rather than avoidant.

Q: Are you using your preferred 'means of escape' as a way to avoid dealing with

1   G. McClure, *"Suicide in Children and Adolescents in England and Wales 1970-1998,"* British Journal of Psychiatry 178 (2001):469-474.

2   https://www.drinkaware.co.uk/alcohol-facts/drinking-habits-and-behaviours/binge-drinking/, accessed September 10, 2016; NHS Choices, Binge Drinking, http://www.nhs.uk/Livewell/alcohol/Pages/Bingedrinking.aspx, accessed September 10, 2016

personal issues or problems? What are you reluctant to deal with at the moment?

[your response]

But even the so-called extroverts wear masks, often to hide their sadness or depression. We wear masks when we presume that our authentic emotions or opinions will not be valued and once voiced, we will be rejected. What so many suicidal people fail to realise is that the world is desperately in need of the authentic; it is saturated with fakes and pretence copycats. We do the world and ourselves a disservice by being a phoney. So often we seek to escape from the sobering truth of who we really are.

Sobriety is not just about abstinence from alcohol. There are many activities or substances which would dull the mind if engaged in or consumed to excess. For example, the tv and film industries encourage us to live in an alternate reality. When real life gets too tough, boring or exasperating, we tune in or click on to an alternate reality (alternative to our own) where other peoples' lives seem more interesting, exciting, straightforward or fulfilling than our own. The deception of such art-forms is that for a brief moment in time, we think we're somewhere else - transported from your own reality.

Care needs to be taken to spend more time in actual rather than virtual reality. We need to get used to reality, learn to deal with its everyday challenges, instead of seeking to escape through virtual reality and fantasy. It's what makes life interesting and adventurous, and what builds character.

Q: Do you feel so overwhelmed by bad news in your own life or through the internet, newspapers, radios and tv that you habitually retreat into fantasy?

[your response]

On the face of it, focusing on others and forgetting ourselves is a positive and humane way of leading our lives; we can gain a certain measure of satisfaction from extending empathy and consideration to those in our circle of friends and acquaintances as well as strangers in need. However, to have our empathy evoked solely by on-screen performances or news of far-flung calamities rather than face-to-face, direct human interactions, means there is no useful outlet for our emotions. Sadly, we have become too addicted to screens in our modern age. As such we prefer to do relationships from behind the safety of a screen.

Q: When last did you truly feel moved by another's problem or circumstances? How did it influence your outlook on your own life?

[your response]

Chapter 12

Drug-induced Suicidal Urges

Patients with mental health concerns such as depression are likely to be prescribed psychoactive medication, many of which pose a risk of suicide - thinking or planning. Some drugs produce terrible side effects such as psychosis or delirium, far worse than the conditions they seek to treat. Because the effect of a drug on an individual is largely unpredictable, it is only through self-reporting on a wider scale that such severe, life-threatening side effects can come to the attention of those who have the power to take those drugs in question off the market. However, if you are on such medication, you may not be aware of how much it may be adversely affecting you.

Psychiatry has 'medicalised' ordinary emotions such as fear and anxiety which were formerly considered part of the complex web of normal human emotions. Depression is defined clinically according to the Diagnostic and statistical Manual of the American Psychiatric Association, 5th edition [DSM-5] categories. For example, to warrant a diagnosis of a major depressive disorder or clinical depression, single episode, a person must have experienced five of the nine symptoms below for at least two weeks as a change from his usual behaviour:

1. Depressed or irritable mood.

2. Significant loss of interest or pleasure in most activities.

3. A considerable loss or gain of weight when not dieting.

4. Difficulty falling or staying asleep, or sleeping more than usual.

5. Behaviour that is observed to be agitated or slowed down.

6. Fatigue or diminished energy.

7. Thoughts of worthlessness or extreme guilt.

8. Reduced ability to think, concentrate or make decisions.

9. Frequent thoughts of death or suicide or attempted suicide.

These criteria correlate with The International

Statistical Classification of Diseases and Related Health Problems, 10th edition [ICD-10] where a depressive episode is defined in section F32 as follows:[1]

In typical mild, moderate, or severe depressive episodes, the patient suffers from lowering of mood, reduction of energy, and decrease in activity. Capacity for enjoyment, interest, and concentration is reduced, and marked tiredness after even minimum effort is common. Sleep is usually disturbed and appetite diminished. Self-esteem and self-confidence are almost always reduced and, even in the mild form, some ideas of guilt or worthlessness are often present. The lowered mood varies little from day to day, is unresponsive to circumstances and may be accompanied by so-called "somatic" symptoms, such as loss of interest and pleasurable feelings, waking in the morning several hours before the usual time, depression worst in the morning, marked psychomotor retardation, agitation, loss of appetite, weight loss, and loss of libido.

The medical model of diagnosis and treatment

---

1   ICD-10,   http://apps.who.int/classifications/icd10/browse/2016/ en#/F32.0, accessed September 26, 2016.

sees suicidal behaviour as linked to low serotonin levels in the brain. All the depression categories are deemed to be mood disorders which necessitate pharmaceutical intervention.

Although the European Medicines Agency recommends that the first line of treatment for moderate to severe depression be talking therapy, waiting lists in the UK can be as long as 18 months. In the meantime, doctors may feel obliged to prescribe medicine such as Prozac (a Selective Serotonin Re-uptake Inhibitor) which can have harmful side effects.

Q: Do you sense that your psychiatric medication may be heightening your anxiety? What symptoms have you been feeling which are different from before you started taking them?

[your response]

Kilpatrick, the author of 'Psychological Seduction: the Failure of Modern Psychology' sees depression as a form of self-pre-occupation which leads to despair. The depressive retreats into his own world, then asks *"if this is all there is to life, why carry on?"*[1]

The medical model, with its emphasis on assessment of pathology or symptoms, diagnosis, and treatment or cure, does not focus on the relationship between the distressed person and the helper which is so crucial in suicide prevention. The tendency to treat a broken spirit like a broken leg will mean that the problem only gets bandaged. Somatic treatments such as psycho-active medication and physical exercise may help to relieve symptoms of depression and anxiety but are limited because they do not address the underlying causation, whether physical or spiritual, thereby prolonging the patients' distress.

Often, with psychoactive medication, the patient experiences the added burden of dealing with physical or psychological side-effects. Furthermore,

---

1   William kirk Kilpatrick, Psychological seduction: the Failure of Modern Psychology (Naashville, Camden, New York: Thomas Nelson Publishers, 1983), 68.

the modern medical tendency to link all human dysfunction to faulty genes does not address the fact that genes cannot predetermine behaviour but can only prescribe a range of possible reactions to a given stimulus.

In many cases drugs have the capacity to blur our perception of reality, and even induce suicidal tendencies; so rather than alleviating the anxiety, they compound it.

Melvin Lansky observes that *"depression is the emotional state most commonly and intuitively linked to suicide. But it's unlikely that suicidality results from depression itself as opposed to the patient's shame over his or her depressive preoccupations, disattachments, dysfunctions and burdensomeness within a supportive relationship"*[1]

D. Pilgrim points out that psychiatric diagnoses are cyclical; in other words, symptoms inform a diagnosis of depression, and depression informs the symptoms. He further highlights the fact that 'depression' lacks aetiological and treatment specificity, in other words - causes are not known

---

1   Melvin Lansky, *"Shame and the problem of suicide: a family and systems perspective"* vol. 7, Issue 3 (230-242) 1991, p. 233

and its treatments may be used for other conditions as well.

We must not forget that there are some medical conditions where the individual is not in conscious control of his actions such as schizophrenia and other psychotic disorders. There are also drugs which cause suicidal thinking. Examples would be schizophrenia, and other psychotic disorders.[1] As the patient, you have the power to ask your doctor to review your drugs if they are not agreeing with you. Very few drugs are needed to keep one alive. If you suspect a drug is causing you to have recurring thoughts of suicide, report it to your doctor at once. Your life could be at stake.

1   American Psychiatric Association, Diagnostic and Statistical Manual of Mental Disorders, Fifth Edition, Text Revision (Washington, DC: AMA, 2013), 297.

Part 2 The Insights

"To say yes to life is at one and the same time to say yes to oneself."[1]

---

1   Anonymous

Chapter 1

Looking Beyond Self

Our lives are inextricably linked with others in ways that we cannot fully grasp. As the Apostle Paul wrote - *"No-one lives to himself and no-one dies to himself."*[1]

Q: Do you consider your life to be yours alone, to do with as you please regardless of the impact on others?

[your response]

One mother who lost her daughter to suicide wrote - *"I almost stopped functioning and I could not see how I could ever pick up the pieces of my shattered life and*

---

1   Romans 14:7.

put them together again."[1] What we do and fail to do have a knock-on effect on others, potentially far beyond what we could imagine. People will lose out on what you had to offer, inconsequential though you may have considered it to be.

The following are some responses to the suicide of a loved one:

"…it ripped my life to shreds."

"…when I found out what happened my life came to an end, it stopped and all I do now is exist."

"…time does not release you from the pain you feel."

"…there was a feeling of real searing physical pain inside my heart and grief became full-blown, overwhelming over the months ahead."

"There are so many things we could have shared and done and now they will never happen."

A prevailing message in this world is that human beings are expendable. Yet the fact remains that each human being is of value to someone. We are not isolated beings. Our lives are not truly our own. If we could see how many people have a stake in

1   Quote taken from Survivors of Bereavement by Suicide website with permission, www.uk-sobs.org.uk.

our lives, we would be shocked. If we could grasp how many lives would be impacted by our death, we would be at a loss for words.

Q: Who are those who have invested something meaningful in your life? What did they contribute?

[your response]

The death wish is stronger in some than others. For many it is a mere fleeting thought which goes away as soon as it comes. It was not until Alison Davies, the late pro-life campaigner, travelled to India and was moved by the plight of children who, like her, were disabled - that her death wish was finally silenced. Nothing had changed in terms of her bodily pain and distress. She suffered with spina bifida, hydrocephalus, emphysema, chest infections, arthritis, lordosis, kyphoscoliosis and osteoporosis. She testified that for ten years she wanted to kill herself, and made several attempts to do so. Despite her own severe health problems and disability, she was National Co-ordinator of 'No Less Human'[1] from 1982 until 2013 when she died.

I often read of a trauma or particular challenge suffered by a stranger in the news, and find myself moved to tears; or likewise become strangely inspired by a rare achievement against the odds by strangers although I'm never likely to meet them. Yet, they have left a mark upon my life.

Q: Have you ever found yourself moved by the story of a stranger?

[your response]

---

1   A branch of Society for the Protection of Unborn Children (SPUC) in England.

Suicide affects us all. Whether consciously or not, psychologically vulnerable people who read that someone has died by suicide, may begin to question their own desire to stay alive. This can trigger copycat suicides through what is known as the 'Werther effect'[1].

Theologian, Cyrus Scofield (1842-1921) looked at the incalculable value of human life in terms of the investments made by others into the individual's life. He invites us to - *"Think of the tremendous investment that others have made in your life and mine. For us, mothers have suffered and prayed...fathers have toiled. Teachers have patiently invested years of effort to win us from ignorance into knowledge..."*[2]

Each person needs one person – whether colleague, spouse, parent, sibling, counsellor or friend with whom they can be totally themselves without fear of ridicule. Over the course of your life, the person who performs this function may change from time to time depending on circumstances. This 'confessional' type intimacy (in-to-me-see) is a safety net to prevent us from creating and

1 See Part 1, Chapter 9 'Copycats and Suicide Pacts'

2 C.I. Scofield, *"Is Life worth living?"*, Library of Classic Sermons, newsforchristians.com, accessed August 5 2014.

sustaining false identities.

We can learn to process our negative thoughts and experiences externally with real people we know and trust. However, bear in mind that not all friends or acquaintances can cope with such challenges. In an ideal world, they should be able to spot when we are beginning to believe myths about ourselves such as *"I am ugly"*, *"good for nothing"* or *"I don't know if I can cope any longer"*, and bring them to our attention. However, it is more often the case that close friends and family tend to see us in a rigid, inflexible way simply because we tend to present over time a certain face to those in our inner circle.

Q: Who would you feel most comfortable sharing your thoughts with? If there is no-one within your immediate circle of family, friends and acquaintances, would you consider a 'qualified' stranger?

[your response]

With family and friends, we often struggle to reveal the hidden aspects of ourselves – those which we sense may not meet with their approval. You may find it easier to share your difficult and overwhelming thoughts with a stranger, although there is much courage required for this as well.

In Japan, a scheme was organised by city officials and professional psychologists whereby hairdressers are being recruited to work alongside counsellors in relating to suicidal patients.[1] What the hairdressers were most valued for was their ability to lend a listening ear.

If you are human, your existing thought pattern is basically self-centred. As you read this sentence, there are an array of disparate thoughts which might be whizzing around your head such as: *"what will I have for lunch? Will I be able to pay my bills? Where should I go on holiday this year? I hope I pass my exams!"* The common theme in these thoughts is *"I"*. It is not necessarily the thoughts themselves, but the human tendency to be self-preoccupied at the expense of others; our natural preoccupation is with *"me, myself and I"*. This explains

1   Danielle Demetriou, *"Feel Suicidal? Come in for a haircut,"* Daily Telegraph (London), November 1, 2010.

why people persist with an addictive behaviour even though it is undermining their health and posing a risk to others' health, have an affair even though they know it will hurt their spouse and damage their relationship; and ultimately kill themselves even though they may know they are ducking out of life's challenges and they will leave a trail of sorrow.

To be able to determine the timing and manner of your death when your life seems to be spinning out of control, may appear to be the only thing you have left which you can control. Clearly, it is the fear of being out of control which is the driving factor. But the reality is that being out of control is a factor all humans must accept.

Q: Have you considered looking at your life
     in terms of what you can contribute rather
     than what you can control? How does this
     change your outlook?

[your response]

Chapter 2

Experiencing a Paradigm Shift

Whatever philosophy you hold about life will either strengthen or weaken your resolve to live. Consider Shakespeare's hero Macbeth who, in the face of adversity railed against his fate as follows:

> *"Life's but a walking shadow, a poor player,*
> *that struts and frets his hour upon the stage*
> *, and then is heard no more . It is a tale told*
> *by an idiot, full of sound and fury, signifying*
> *nothing."*[1]

Q: What metaphor would you use to compare your life to?

For example, is life:

A bed of roses?

A steep mountain climb?

A walk in the park?

A treadmill?

A revolving door?

1   Macbeth, Act 5, Scene 5, 24-28.

[your response]

As stated so poignantly by William Kilpatrick, Professor of Educational Psychology, "... *every instinct in us tells us this is not the place we were meant for. As a station on the way, as a temporary rest for weary travellers, we can accept it and even love it. But as the only place, as the final destination, it represents ultimate frustration.*"[1]

Q: What are some of the ways you have been avoiding difficult aspects of your life?

[your response]

---

1   William Kirk Kilpatrick, 'Psychological Seduction: The Failure of Modern Psychology' (Nashville, Camden, New York: Thomas Nelson Publishers, 1983), 133.

The classic Hollywood movie plot is centred on the premise that the general public does not want to watch a storyline which mirrors their own experiences; rather they want to escape into a fantasy world that is so far removed from their reality that they can in effect forget their lives for a few hours. It begs the question as to why we should want to escape from our inner selves in this mind-numbing and superficial way when time is our most precious commodity. We forget how fleeting time is, and how little of it we may actually have left.

It is unrealistic to think we can be happy all the time. There is a lot about the human condition that awakens anger and sadness. The writer of Ecclesiastes bemoaned the fact that *"...what is crooked cannot be made straight, and what is lacking cannot be numbered."*[1]

Q: Could it be that God put you on this earth to lessen the misery rather than add to it? In what ways could you contribute to lessening human misery?

[your response]

---

1 Ecclesiastes 1:15.

So often we look at what's wrong with the world, and feel like victims; but we can choose differently – to look at the world from the point of view of a 'trouble-shooter'.

Most human beings when they see trouble coming, head in the opposite direction. That would seem the most sensible thing to do. Yet, trouble is an inevitable aspect of living. If we spent our whole lives running away from trouble, what quality of life would we have? Sooner or later, we must face trouble head on as this is the only way we can ever hope to find a solution.

You have to get to the point where you determine - *"well, if I have to die in the process of going through whatever it is I'm currently facing, so be it; but I'm not going to bow out without a fight!"*

We humans are so skilled at avoiding trouble that we have developed diverse ways of doing so.

Q: Can you relate to some of these ways? Examples are listed below:

Claiming hypochondria (a disorder characterised by baseless, imagined illness) to avoid responsibilities.

Indulging in drugs or alcohol to numb the mind.

Overdosing on media entertainment to escape from reality.

Sports obsession to experience a sense of victory against the odds, albeit vicariously.

[your response]

We're so afraid of trouble that we imagine it when it's not there or so blow it out of proportion, as to end up in hospital with hypertension, ulcers or worse physical conditions. Ironically, we are very good at bringing trouble on ourselves even though it is the very thing we are seeking so desperately to avoid.

So why would God let you be born for trouble? Job asked this ultimate existential question in the aftermath of unimaginable loss. In a single day, he lost his 10 children, 7,000 sheep, 3,000 camels, 500 yoke of oxen, 500 female donkeys and servants. From the abyss of his grief, he questioned his very existence -

> *"Why is light given to him who is in misery, and life to the bitter of soul, who long for death but it does not come...?"*[1]

Perhaps, trouble is a tool God allows for a higher purpose. Perhaps, if there were no trouble, we would not seek God and yearn for a perfect world. Perhaps, that is the purpose of each life - to strive for and accomplish something which will make the world a bit more like the place it was always supposed to be. Perhaps, we must pay a huge price, just as God paid a huge price, before the perfect world He intended, can be restored. Perhaps, in the grand scheme of things, trouble was never meant to defeat us but define us – making us the people we were always meant to be.

---

1   Job 3:20.

Chapter 3

Guarding Your Mind

Although there is only one external world of human reality, individuals create their own world through their unique perceptions, thoughts and attitudes. These shape what we experience of the external world. Our thoughts and perceptions shape how we see the outside world. The external world is constantly trying to invade the internal. It is vital to establish mental guards - *"guard your heart with all diligence because out of it springs the issues of life."*[1]

Cyberbullying is just one example of how cruel the outside world can be. Bullies seek a perverse sense of superiority by trying to trying to make others feel inferior. The best form of defence is internal – simply refusing to believe what they say about you. Social media is being used in anti-social ways to try to demean those who are considered 'different' in some way or as a way to gain a false sense of superiority. Our minds also need a 'safe place' to retreat to when our interior worlds suffer an invasion which causes us to recoil in shock,

1   Proverbs 4:23, KJV.

horror, disgust. It is important not to become so caught up in life's everyday demands that we fail to define and cultivate that 'safe place' for ourselves. In essence, we can decide just how much of the external world to let in.

Sometimes when life is difficult, we tend to reminisce about the past and wonder if our lives would be better now if we had taken a different route. The truth is that if you had chosen differently, so many other things and people would have been different as well. Hence there is absolutely no telling where you could have been by now. I don't know which is more unsettling - the thought of what might have been or what will be; but if I had to make a choice which to dwell on, it would definitely be the latter because tomorrow is still all to play for whereas yesterday is done and dusted.

Q: What is your biggest regret in life? What can you learn from it to enable you to move forward?

[your response]

Human knowledge can be overwhelming. It is possible that a depressed person has contemplated a problem to a nauseating extent yet still remains conflicted about what is the right decision. King Solomon summed it up as *"the more knowledge, the more grief."*[1] We are living in the information age where knowledge proliferates at an exponential rate. The internet has been a major contributor, putting literally vast amounts of knowledge at our fingertips. For example, Marjorie Wallace, Chief Executive of the mental health charity, SANE, has noted that websites promoting suicide are easily accessible and *"preying on vulnerable and lonely people."*[2]

Added to this is the popular press with its focus on the negative happenings in the world - natural disasters, poverty, sickness and human neglect and cruelty. It is easy for those who are suicidal to be swept along on the tide of negative information which leads to negative thinking.

Q: Who or what is the biggest influence on your frame of mind?

---

1   Ecclesiastes 1:18.

2   BBC News: Health, *"Fears over pro-suicide web pages,"* www.bbc. co.uk, accessed April 11, 2008.

[your response]

You can discover how to take responsibility for your own life and be able to interpret what happens to you in life in ways which do not lead to self-destruction.

Feelings are by their very nature illogical. As human beings, we are subject to fluctuating emotions, often unjustifiable and unaccountable. But the essence of knowing yourself is to be aware of these fluctuations. Sometimes you may not have a clue how you are feeling at any given moment or you may have difficulty admitting your feelings even to yourself. However, you can consciously decide to create positive thoughts and attitudes about life. This is not always straightforward. For example, factors such as psychoactive medication or and sleep patterns might be controlling your mind without your realising it.

Without our feelings, we would be 'zombies' without initiative because these same emotions are the source of our motivation. We can be fully aware of what we should have done, ought to do and could do, but what actually gets done is usually a direct result of our feelings at the time. This human dichotomy is eloquently conveyed in the statement - *"I do not understand my own actions. For I do not do what I want, but I do the very thing I hate."*[1] Nevertheless, our emotions are not the source of our problems. It's how we choose to act on our emotions that produce either a positive or negative result.

Q: When last did you feel strongly about something? What action or response resulted from this feeling?

[your response]

---

1   Romans 7:15.

Every emotion can be harnessed for our own good or the good of others, if we exercise caution and foresight instead of acting recklessly. Common reckless behaviours include driving too fast, firing a gun in anger, reaching for junk food in frustration or swallowing an overdose of pills in despair.

There is a difference between feelings and wants, though the way we use these terms may lead to confusion. For example, if you say 'I feel as if I want to have a bath', you are feeling possibly hot, dirty, itchy. The desire to have a bath is your preferred way though not the only way of responding to this feeling, and involves a decision. The original statement dilutes your intention, indicating a certain ambivalence in your choice. If you had said 'I want to have a bath' or 'I'm going to have a bath', the choice you made in response to your feelings, would be clearer.

Q: What strong emotions have you experienced recently? What different ways did you act on the same feeling?

[your response]

Here are ten illustrations of how different people respond to the same feeling of anger - go to the gym; verbalise abuse; kill someone; commit vandalism; lobby an organization; take hostages; watch a comedy on tv; pray; binge eat; attempt suicide.

It may be the case that certain people make up their minds to kill themselves as a way to stop the constant barrage of negative thinking. First and foremost, don't be afraid of your thoughts, but rather seek to process them in a methodical way. Try writing down how you feel, then ask yourself why you feel this way. Finally, ask yourself, what would be a positive way to deal with these feelings.

Q: What positive step can you take
      immediately?

[your response]

Chapter 4

Discovering Your Purpose

We've been sold the lie that human life is dispensable. After all, so the reasoning goes, there are over seven billion souls on the planet. The film *'It's a Wonderful Life'* demonstrates how one man's life had a knock-on effect on so many others such that when his guardian angel played the show reel of what life in his sleepy town would have been like had he never been born, the town was completely unrecognisable for all the wrong reasons. Take heart from the fact that if lived to its highest potential, your life will make an incalculable difference to the people around you.

Q: What is the difference only you can make?

[your response]

St. Anthony, when tasked with responding appropriately to a blind man's question - *"can there be anything worse than losing your eye sight?"*, replied, *"yes, losing your vision."*[1] Inner vision is of far greater importance than physical sight. This allows you to see yourself in the near and distant future, inspired by a noble pursuit which enables you to rise above the petty annoyances and distractions of everyday life.

Q: What is the one thing you could genuinely live for or throw yourself into whole-heartedly?

The answer could be a person, a project or a cause.

[your response]

---

1   'Prayables: 10 Sayings for the happy life,' beliefnet.com, accessed September 26, 2016.

Life becomes truly worth living when we pursue the life we were born to live, not the life we think we should have because we think that's how everyone else is living; nor the life our parents wish us to live because that's the way they have lived and consider best; much less the life society is projecting as the ultimate ideal. Without a deep sense of knowing we are on the right track or headed in the right direction, we will be filled with a restlessness or dissatisfaction that leaves us more prone to poor judgement and defeatist decision-making such as the decision to end our lives.

Hollywood has succeeded in foisting its value system based on materialism, greed, and hedonism upon most other cultures through the film and tv industries. These values are celebrated as the gateway to maximising quality of life and satisfaction. You may have swallowed the lie that this too is what you should be aspiring to. You are free to decide your own way.

To illustrate how insidious the dissemination of these values can be, we need look no further than the modern media. The overwhelming media focus on celebrities, and constant celebrity self-promotion, undoubtedly results in a large number of the general public feeling as if they are relatively insignificant.

It is important to recognise that the news is not just something out there beyond your control. You create news minute by minute through your actions and decisions. Your news may not hit the headlines or front page of a national newspaper, but it is important nonetheless.

We are encouraged by the imbalanced focus of the media, to evaluate and celebrate people based on superficial qualities such as wealth, award-winning achievement and outward appearance. If we are lacking in these qualities, we may conclude that our lives are insignificant. We all influence one another in countless ways, and how we choose to live our lives impacts on others.

The vital truth has been overlooked that, even when aspects of our physical lives and circumstances disappoint us, we can all nurture and share those qualities which make for good character and a happy society such a smile, good manners, mutual respect and kindness.

Part 3 The Keys

"Anyone desperate enough for suicide should be desperate enough to go to creative extremes to solve problems: elope at midnight stow away on the boat to New Zealand and start over, do what they always wanted to do but were afraid to try."[1]

---

1   Richard Bach, 1936.

Key 1

Think and act in ways which nurture hope.

I hope so far this book has already convinced you that there is good reason to be hopeful. Your worth most certainly cannot and should not be defined by anything outside yourself such as your material possessions, relationships or social status. They can all be taken away from you. You can even lose parts of your body or your mind.

Without hope, it is pointless to do most things in life which make life worth living. Human beings can endure a mammoth amount of stress, pain and discomfort if they can grasp just an iota of hope for a brighter tomorrow.

David Webb, former suicide attempter and suicide researcher, discovered for himself that he was much more than the sum total of his thoughts and gained liberation from his suicidal thinking once he challenged Descarte's belief that *"I think, therefore I am"*. He discovered it to be the opposite

– "*I am, therefore I think.*" It became possible for him to contemplate an existence in spite of the fact that his thinking was often out of wack and self-sabotaging. David Webb credits "*spiritual self-inquiry*" with saving his life.[1]

Dare to consider some thought-provoking questions and embark on some soul-searching.

Q: What would you say has been the highlight of your life so far?

[your response]

Even in a weak state or at a seeming disadvantage, a living person is in a position where a breakthrough could occur, and so is in a stronger position than a dead person who was once considered strong. As long as there is life, there is always the opportunity

1   David Webb, "*The Many Languages of Suicide,* "http://jungcircle. com/DWebb.html, accessed September 2, 2016

for your situation or outlook to improve with time. It is hope which enables a person to persevere in the midst of hardship, and not to give up.

Hope is a constituent of faith. Faith is defined by the author of Hebrews as *"the substance of things hoped for, the evidence of things not seen."*[1] Essentially what is hoped for cannot be seen with your physical eyes although you may be able to see it in your imagination, and so hope is an essential component of faith.

A suicidal mind may be trapped in the misconception that life will always remain the way it is, unaware that it is his perception that is stuck. There will therefore seem no point in carrying on. But just as nature experiences seasons which ebb and flow, your life will also be subject to seasonal changes.

In a world full of bad news, aim to build up your empty or depleted reserves of hope by collecting awe-inspiring stories of transformation and defying the odds. Here are two which worked for me:

A baby born at just 25 weeks defied all medical

1   Hebrews 11:1.

prognosis of death even though he weighed less than a bag of sugar.[1]

A stranger offered sufficient hope to derail the suicidal plans of a young man poised to jump off Waterloo Bridge in 2008. You may wonder what exactly the good Samaritan said which caused the desperate young man to change his mind? He approached him with the following words:

> *"... please don't do this ... you can get better. Let's have a cup of coffee and we can talk about this."*[2]

1   Anna Hodgekiss, MailOnline, http://www.dailymail.co.uk/health/article-2897183/Couple-told-abort-non-viable-baby-son-mother-s-waters-broke-just-20-weeks-celebrate-birthday-ignoring-doctors-advice.html, accessed February 27, 2015.

2   Tara Brady and Amanda Williams, MailOnline, *"'I've found Mike' – suicidal man whose life was saved by a stranger ... Find Mike"*, accessed January 30, 2014.

Key 2

Re-consider not just the load you are carrying but how you are carrying it.

Marcus Aurelius, Roman Emperor from 161 – 180, wrote - *"Do not disturb yourself by thinking of the whole of your life. Do not let your thoughts at once embrace all the various troubles which you may expect to befall you; but on every occasion ask yourself, 'What is there in this which is intolerable and past bearing?' ... remember that neither the future nor the past claims you, but only the present."*[1]

Too heavy a load carried for too long will lead to overload and cause you to dread future loads. A good analogy would be weight training, the weights are necessary to trigger the growth of muscles but it is important to build your weight resistance gradually or you could injure yourself.

Q: Are you suffering from overload by trying to do too much ?

---

1   Marcus Aurelius, Translated by George Long, 'The Meditations', classics.mit.edu, accessed September 26, 2016.

[your response]

One suicide attempter in England attributed her suicidal urges to the fact that *"I was just trying to squeeze too much into my life and didn't know when to stop."*[1]

There is a need to keep a proper balance between work and play, the material and the spiritual. Those who are workaholics or relationship addicts may be consumed with one aspect of their lives to the neglect of others. This one dimension of their lives becomes their sole purpose for living often without their realising it. It is only when something goes wrong in this one area such as a redundancy or relationship let-down that the lack of balance may

1 Jilly Beattie, 'By Killing Myself I Felt I Was Saving My Baby From Life of Misery With Me,' The Mirror (London, England), April 17, 2007 in Questia Online Library, http://www.questia.com/read/5020312043, accessed October 15, 2009

come to light. Alternatively, they may be trying to do too much, and ignoring their bodies' need for rest and relaxation.

Strive to keep your life in balance. You can do so by:

Dividing the day into 3 parts: morning afternoon, night.

Focusing on the three highest priorities:

Examples are:

God, family, ministry.

Spiritual, physical, social.

Work, family, health.

Q: What are the tasks you need to do in each category of the three you've chosen?

[your response]

Life can be hard but it was never meant to be unbearable. When you start sensing you are approaching breaking point, consider letting go of things and avoid taking on any new responsibilities or activities. The irony is that loss is often gain, and less is often more. Whatever you allow into your inner world must be only that which will enhance your ability to hear the voice of God and inspire you to embrace your inner ideals. Only take from life what is necessary to help you blossom into your true self.

Key 3

Ditch the pressurised, wearisome or superficial activities which ultimately leave you feeling empty.

It is possible that diminishing job satisfaction or persistent job dissatisfaction could mean that the work you have undertaken simply is not right for you rather than you are not right for the job. By looking at this dilemma from the former perspective, you save yourself from the need to berate yourself for being inadequate or defective. Even if you cannot leave your job immediately, begin to formulate a strategy for finding a more rewarding alternative. Let your long-term goal be to do work which stimulates and fulfils you, and not just enables you to pay the bills. Stress and lack of job satisfaction are amongst factors which have been implicated in work-related depression and suicides.[1]

It could be that you are spending too little time

1   "*Crying Shame*", Hazards 101 January-March, 2008, www.hazards.org/suicide/cryingshame.htm.

outdoors in nature and the fresh air, and too much time in enclosed buildings in front of computer screens. This is a contributing factor in workplace stress.

Try your best to enjoy your work even if it's just one small aspect. Taking pleasure in your work will prevent over-pre-occupation with the passage of time. You may be spending an inordinate amount of time at work or in a high-pressure job. Even if your job is not very demanding, the sense of pressure may result from a fear of job loss or letting down family members, employers or colleagues.

Q: Do you feel that your entire identity is defined by work? What is missing?

[your response]

Recognise that you are not your job title, status or

pay cheque; it is simply what you do. Be aware of the signs that the job may be taking over your life such as insomnia, a prolonged lack of proper work/ life balance and suicidal thinking. Ultimately, recognise that the job is replaceable but your life is not.

It is also possible to suffer an over-kill of leisure and pleasure. After the initial pleasure factor has worn off, you may conclude that life is meaningless because a sense of true fulfilment still proves elusive. Indeed, human beings can weary themselves by looking for new thrills to excite and entertain. Although this may gratify the five physical senses, it will not satisfy the deep longings of your soul. Soul satisfaction comes from seeking God and spiritual truth with your whole heart rather than seeking the material pleasures of life.

Key 4

Cultivate a long-term vision for your life.

As illogical as it may appear, it is possible to decide to be positive in spite of unfavourable external conditions. If you've been struggling with a problem all your life, it's difficult to imagine what it would be like to be free of it. For the suicidal mind, all life presents is a big black hole where all is negative.

But, there is always something positive even if all you can say is *"it could have been worse!"* You will need to decide what will make you want to live even when life is tough.

Q: Be honest – where would you like to be in five, ten, twenty years from now?

[your response]

You can cultivate the habit of visualising the future you desire through panoramic, long lenses. After all, long-term goals encourage perseverance and durability. Abraham was told by the Lord to *"Lift your eyes now and look from the place where you are – northward, southward, eastward, and westward..."*[1]

Without a deep sense of knowing you are on the right track or headed in the right direction, you will be prone to restlessness which in turn can predispose you to poor decision-making and judgement such as suicidal thinking and planning.

It is good to engage in planning, writing lists and building vision boards as a way of keeping your mind focused on your goals and less prone to distractions.

Q: Do you become prone to distress and disillusioned when things do not turn out the way you had planned? Give a recent example.

[your response]

---

1 Genesis 13:14.

Patience can be viewed as the opposite of pride because the proud insist that things must go their way when they want them to, and if they don't, they may then be unable to cope with reality. The suicidal act may then constitute an avoidance of reality.

"The patient in spirit is better than the proud in spirit ... do not hasten in your spirit to be angry, for anger rests in the bosom of fools."[1]

Patience may also be considered as the opposite of anger. Ecclesiastes shows the connection between pride and anger. God questioned Jonah's anger:

"But it displeased Jonah exceedingly, and he became angry. So he prayed to the Lord, and said, 'Ah, Lord, was not this what I said when I was still in my country? Therefore I fled previously to Tarshish; for I know that You are a gracious and merciful God, slow to anger and abundant in lovingkindness, One who relents from doing harm. Therefore now, O Lord, please take my life from me, for it is better for me to die than to live!' Then the Lord said, 'Is it right for you to be

---

1   Ecclesiastes 7:8-9.

angry?"'[1]

Jonah expressed being angry enough to die which confirms that anger taken to its full extent can lead to self-destruction.

You can spare yourself much misery by recognising that the road to your goals will never be easy. There will be unavoidable delays, road-blocks, breakdowns, and the like, but if you keep the faith and persist, you will reach your destination even though the journey often seems unbearably slow or to have come to a standstill.

It is difficult if not impossible to understand the trajectory of our lives until the end when God will make everything clear. Apostle Paul states that *"for now we see in a mirror dimly but then face to face. Now I know in part, then I shall know fully, even as I have been fully known."*[2]

Often hopes and dreams make take longer than expected to come to fruition. To be quick to anger may lead to self-destruction[3], which means you

---

1   Jonah 4:1-4.

2   1 Corinthians 13:12.

3   Ecclesiastes 7:8-9.

would never discover all the good eventualities awaiting you around the corner.

Key 5

Accept yourself - warts and all.

You are the one whom you spend all your time with. Friends and family only visit. They can't get inside your head unless you let them in, but you live there permanently. Is it a nice place to be?

Q: What pattern of thoughts are you having?

[your response]

Record your voice using the following positive affirmations. Your mind may struggle to believe what you're reading but pretend for a moment you are a highly paid actor. Assume a cheerful tone. Play the recording back to yourself at least three times a day:

- *"I am valuable to the world."*

- *"I am loved."*

- *"I am capable."*

- *"I have a lot to offer."*

Philosopher and Theologian, St Augustine reasoned that the injunction to *"love your neighbour as yourself"* puts the self on par with the neighbour, and so whatever you wouldn't do to your neighbour such as killing, you should also refrain from doing to yourself. In addressing the issue of whether suicide is an act of courage to avoid temptation or trial, Augustine cites the examples of Jesus and the eleven apostles who, in spite of persecution, never resorted to suicide.[1] Why not treat yourself with the same respect and regard you would have for another human being whom you hold in high esteem. Ultimately , to love yourself is to realise that, as valid as your opinions and desires may be, you are a part of a greater whole and it may sometimes be in the common interest to put aside your self-interest .

1   St. Augustine of Hippo, translated by Marcus Dods, The City of God, 426 AD

In this multi-media modern world, we are bombarded by a glut of information about how other people live their lives. But, just because the media puts certain lifestyles on a pedestal doesn't mean they are right for you.

Coveting or envying someone else's life leads to self-rejection. There is no rejection worse, because even if you are rejected by all but accept yourself, there is hope for a new beginning somewhere with a new group of people who will accept you.

Q: Do you often compare your life to others and feel less than?

[your response]

Envy derives from dissatisfaction with oneself and the circumstances of one's life. It is this dissatisfaction which leads to comparison with others, and the view that one is lacking in one attribute or possession.

We are living in an age of comparison, envy and competition. More than ever through the media, we are being granted access into the private lives of others. We begin to think we should have what they have, pursue what they pursue and want what they want. Rather than view it as just another person's choice about how they live, we see it as normative or prescriptive - a commentary on how the masses are living or should be living.

Q: When you think about yourself, what words or images come to mind?

[your response]

There are many things you might want to change about yourself, but also accept that there are good things which do not need to be changed. Self-acceptance is the key to living the life you were meant to live as opposed to the life you're expected to live or think you ought to live. The things which you like least about yourself are often those things which make you unique, and can be a key to what God is calling you to do with your life.

Key 6

Each day, determine to be of service to someone.

You may have believed falsely that what you get from life will determine the quality of your life when in fact the opposite is true. It is what you give of yourself which will bring you the most satisfaction.

Q: When last did you do something kind for someone else?

[your response]

Those who are suicidal, in the vast majority of circumstances have considered their own death not just as a one-off, quick thought just before the act, but over and over again. They may reach the stage where they begin to experience anticipatory grief concerning themselves. It may then become a foregone conclusion that they must die.

Cultivate the practice of empathy by laying aside some time each day to focus all your energy on another human being besides yourself. Find available , pleasant individuals who are willing to talk and engage them in conversation simply by asking them about how life is going for them. Focus on actively listening and ask periodic questions to clarify what they are saying.

This will benefit you enormously be forcing you outside your own mind for a while. You will also begin to see life from other perspectives not just your own. Most surprisingly, you will derive satisfaction from the joy you give to others simply by listening, thereby validating their thoughts and memories.

Q: When last did you do something kind for someone else?

[your response]

Just because you have not yet discovered your value and significance, does not mean you have none.

Key 7

Find an objective and trustworthy person with whom to share your thoughts and feelings.

You may be shying away from sharing your innermost struggles with those closest to you. This is a common human tendency resulting primarily from a fear of ridicule, rejection, disappointing others and loss of privacy. Furthermore, you may have correctly sensed that they wouldn't know how to cope with the feelings you wish to share.

There are many you know who may seek to discount your feelings by trying to talk you out of them. But happiness is not predictable, and feelings are not logical. You may be unhappy for personal reasons which have nothing to do with how your circumstances appear to others. It is only through a meaningful conversation with someone of your choosing that your feelings can find release, and you will find relief from your mental oppression.

It is important not to discount your own thoughts

and feelings by seeking to ignore, deny or suppress them. We may be fearful of sharing your own thoughts; experience may have taught you that they will only be dismissed or belittled. Yet, we were made for sharing. It may interest you to know that when there seems no one else worthy of your secrets, God is always there and that with Him you can freely share all things.

It is very important to process and vent your distress when you experience a crisis rather than just cope by grinning and bearing it. This is not a valid coping mechanism because all this does is suppress your feelings which will eventually lead to your explosion - through angry outbursts or implosion - through depression. By then the damage caused, may be irrecoverable.

Q: Can you think of anyone in your life who can play this role of an active listener?

[your response]

Those who peddle in hope are often pigeonholed into confined categories such as ministers of religion, psychotherapists or motivational speakers. But it is possible for anyone to sense when others' hope is running on empty. We all can be dispensers of hope, but it is not always possible to find someone trustworthy or sensible enough with whom we can share our dilemma or distress, and who can, as it were, present a contrary argument or perspective. We need someone or something to shine a light on our dark thoughts.

Gifts such as singing, dancing, writing and making music are also positive outlets for difficult emotions.

Q: Do you have an artistic gift which might help you process your emotions? When last did you use it?

[your response]

Key 8

Keep a daily journal to increase your self-awareness.

It is all too easy to feel unimportant, even powerless in a world populated by billions who, just like yourself, seek meaning and distinction. It is a foregone conclusion that you are unique because there is not, never has been nor ever will be anyone exactly like you; yet, ironically, you may have spent much of your life preoccupied with trying to prove this known fact. Unfortunately, you may have been divested of your innate sense of self-worth by thoughtless or uncaring adults during our impressionable childhood. You may find yourself desperately trying to regain it, and so prove your worth to others, the result being inner and outer conflict.

Q: What were some of the messages about yourself you received as a child?

[your response]

Counsellor, Dr Ed Welch, stresses the need to distinguish between physical and spiritual symptoms on the basis that *"if we confuse spiritual for physical symptoms, we are liable to ... have little hope for spiritual growth when someone has a psychiatric diagnosis."*[1]

This is important because spiritual/emotional symptoms cannot be rectified by pharmaceutical drugs or any physical intervention. Just because you have a psychiatric diagnosis doesn't mean you cannot get better. If you make the effort to identify and resolve some of the deeper issues within your soul, you will make great progress towards a more satisfying life.

Q: Do you know what symptoms to expect from your diagnosis?

[your response]

---

1   Edward T Welch, 'Blame it on the Brain: distinguishing chemical imbalances, brain disorders, and disobedience' (New Jersey: P&R Publishing, 1988), 119.

Q: Do you know what side effects to expect from your medication?

[your response]

It is helpful to cultivate an awareness of the thoughts and feelings you experience each day.

Dr. Rachel Naomi Remen in her lecture 'the Art of Living every minute of your life'[1] encourages those who wish to regain their love of life to ask themselves the following questions every day:

What surprised me today?

What touched me today?

What inspired me today?

---

1   Remen, Rachel.'The Art of Living Every Minute of Your Life.', Public Lecture, Mini Medical School for the Public from University of California San Francisco,California, March 20, 2008.

A day can make a huge difference in your life. A daily journal will help you to chart your small steps of progress which may otherwise go unnoticed.

Key 9

Decide on an action plan for positive change.

Depressed people usually blame others for their emotions. The alternative is to take responsibility for your emotions – the fact that you have them and can change them. Taking responsibility for your own thoughts, attitudes and feelings means you can break the vicious cycle of assigning blame to someone or something outside yourself, or having to look for solutions outside yourself.

Q: If you are depressed, what do your instincts tell you may be the cause?

[your response]

Deane Alban, author at Naturalnews blog, has identified aspects of the modern lifestyle which may predispose us to depression:

Eating processed food loaded with sugar, unhealthy fats, and additives.

Living in a sea of man-made chemicals - there are over 80,000 in our environment and our food.

Electromagnetic field exposure - the World Health Organization considers cell phones as dangerous as lead and chloroform.

Social isolation

Lack of exercise - most of us spend up to 12 hours per day sitting.

Insomnia - 60% of us regularly don't get enough sleep.

Increased stress.

Increased use of both recreational and prescription drugs.[1]

Q: What role you you consider that any of the

1   Deane Alban, 'Robin Williams and the Growing Epidemic of Depression,' www.naturalnews.com, accessed August 18, 2014

above may be playing in fostering your depression or suicidal urges?

[your response]

Although some people find medication helpful, it does not benefit everyone. Often patients feel medication is the last resort beyond which there is no hope for a solution.

Q: Do you feel hopeless because your medication is not working or is making you feel worse?

[your response]

Life is about change. Accepting change is not always easy as it is often accompanied by the loss of things which we feel make our life worthwhile. We are all works-in-progress and we allow growth in our lives when we nurture a 'growth' as opposed to a 'fixed' mind-set.

Q: What have you lost in your life which makes the future seem impossible without it?

[your response]

Although you may not have realised it, your primary relationship is with yourself. David Webb has described suicide as 'a crisis of the self'.

Q: In what ways have you been ignoring or dismissing the signs of this impending crisis?

[your response]

Below are some examples of signs and examples which others who were suicidal have experienced:

Lack of concern about personal welfare.

- unkempt dressing

Changes in social pattern.

- cancelling social engagements.

Decline in work productivity or school achievement.

- malingering, calling in sick or worsening grades at school.

Alterations in sleep and eating patterns.

- over-eating or sleeping less

Attempts to put personal matters in order or to make amends with others

- *making a will, reaching out to friends and family*

Preoccupation with themes of death and violence.

- *curiosity about the after-life, collecting articles or borrowing books on death and dying.*

Sudden improvement in mood after a period of depression.

- *a burst of energy and desire to do things because, after much ambivalence, you have finally decided to end your life .*

Q: Are you aware of what makes you anxious?

[your response]

Dr. Bill Knaus, contributor at Psychology Today, has identified that *"perfectionism is a common trigger for anxiety."*[1]

If you begin to change your priorities and view the significant aspect of your life as participation and not achievement, this will help to enhance your enjoyment and relive you of the pressure to always excel in whatever you do.

If some situation is causing you undue anxiety or discomfort, consider how you can get out of it, make the best of it or ensure you never get yourself into that situation again. These are empowering thoughts which energise rather than paralyse you.

Above all, life is about change. Changes are required on either of two levels - knowing how to adjust to it when it is thrust upon you , and knowing when to initiate it. If you don't initiate necessary changes in your life - changes that foster your maturity - events will conspire to force you to change. Strive to take back some control of your life by initiating necessary changes rather than having changes foisted on you.

1   *"What can we learn from Comedian Robin Williams' suicide?"* Science and Sensibility, www.psychologytoday.com, accessed 29 December 2014.

Key 10

Train your mind to focus only on the positive.

To simplify your life involves internal and external de-cluttering. There may be things you are doing which are simply feeding your despair. For example, do you need to turn off the news?

Q: Did you read or hear any bad news recently that deflated or depressed you?

[your response]

You may not be as impervious to bad news as you might think. There is only so much bad news any one person can take. Depending on which articles or newspapers you read, you can either feel inspired, encouraged, depressed or devastated.

Also, the underlying messages in many lifestyle magazines are:

'You are not good enough as you are'

'You need to buy this product to be happy or complete.'

Instead of giving up on life, there are things you would do well to give up in terms of long-held attachments to things which are effectively killing your desire to live. These may be:

Perceptions.

Ideologies.

Relationships.

Lifestyles.

Q: Is there anything you would like to add to this list or wish to specify in each of the categories which may apply to you?

[your response]

Circumstances may sometimes appear to rob you of choice, yet in any giving trauma or tragedy, the choice may be made to focus on the one or two good things rather than the seemingly surpassing negative things.

Q: What is the one positive thing in your life you can identify?

[your response]

Key 11

Ensure your world view, core values and guiding principles affirm life.

For the next 1 minute, aim to think only positive thoughts. To help you keep on track, it might be useful to record your thoughts by using a digital device or writing them down.

[your response]

Each day aim to begin and end the day in this way. Each week you can lengthen the time by 1 minute or as you feel able.

Start a gratitude journal, and each day write at least one thing about your life for which you are grateful.

Immediate solutions may prove elusive but a positive perspective will enable you to either manage or overcome your circumstances instead of your circumstances overcoming you. You stand to lose nothing and gain so much just from remaining resolutely positive even in the face of grim realities.

Q: Have you incurred a huge debt which it seems may take a lifetime, to pay off?

[your response]

This may be a financial debt or a moral debt which comes from having offended or caused someone harm or grief. You may attempt to silence or drown out the voice of conscience through such means as drugs, alcohol or entertainment. The ultimate silence is through suicide.

Q: What do you believe about God and the role He plays in humanity?

[your response]

Here are five Bible-based statements about God. If you choose to meditate on them daily, they will change your perception of the challenges you may be facing:

- God exists.

- He rewards those who dilligently seek Him.

- He is working all things for good, even what seems evil, in the lives of His faithful followers.

- God only allows in our lives the burdens we can bear, and He helps us carry them.

- All human suffering is temporary.

Q: If you were to frame a motto / guiding principle for your life, what would it be?

[your response]

Key 12

Seek to find and live your purpose, not what is expected of you, popular or merely within your capabilities.

You may have never considered that you have a purpose which is unique to you. No career guidance counsellor, parent or teacher can tell you what this is, you must discover it for yourself.

Every human-being has at least one talent , and that is really all that is necessary. A multi-talented individual will be faced with the choice of which talent to nurture first because to achieve anything, you will have to be focused on that one thing for a considerable period of time.

Even the weak, down-and-out and disabled possess at least one talent or strength, be it so seemingly small as the ability to make others laugh or an eye for detail. So far, you may have struggled to identify your talent or true vocation in life , but the answer lies simply in tuning into your intuition and listening to your inner voice. The problem is that we are disconnected from this 'voice' and more tuned into the 'voice of reason' (other peoples' expectations and opinions). Intuition (messages embedded in thoughts and feelings) is one of God's way of communicating with us. We often ignore our intuition because what it tells us may seem too difficult or to follow it would be too uncomfortable a leap of faith. For example, if you have a parent who wants you to pursue a career in Accounting, but you have a strong pull towards the Creative Arts and the thought of Accounting fills you with horror or repulsion, that is your intuition speaking.

Think of yourself as the pilot of your life. No pilot of sound mind would dare fly a plane without links to the control tower, yet so many of us embark on a life without close communication with our Creator. The 'take-control-of -your-life' credo of modern, western thinking tends to give us an exaggerated sense of our own capabilities. On life's journey, we all need a compass to keep us headed in the right direction. We can choose money, fame, good looks, drugs, education but they will all eventually disappoint for only what is of eternal value can satisfy forever. Too often, we choose diversions that lead us off-track from our destinations or where we're destined to be. You may sense you are off-track but you cannot re-route without knowing where you are headed.

Q: How might your life be different by viewing it as a search for something different such as enlightenment, insight or wisdom rather than material acquisitions?

[your response]

You may have cultivated a convenient habit of underestimating your abilities with a false sense of humility. Humility can be best described as 'thinking of ourselves less, not thinking less of ourselves'.

You may play various roles in society but seek to identify that one overarching purpose which defines who you are. You should be able to fit all your individual roles under this umbrella.

Q: Here are three questions which will guide
     you in finding your purpose:

What do I see myself doing?

How do I see myself being?

Where do I see myself ending up?

[your response]

The 12 Life Affirming Keys.

Key 1:   Think and act in ways which nurture hope.

Key 2:   Re-consider not just the load you are carrying but how you are carrying it.

Key 3:   Ditch the pressurised, wearisome or superficial activities which ultimately leave you feeling empty.

Key 4:   Cultivate a long-term vision for your life.

Key 5:   Accept yourself -warts and all.

Key 6:   Each day, determine to be of service to someone.

Key 7:   Find an objective and trustworthy person with whom to share your thoughts and feelings.

Key 8:   Keep a daily journal to increase your self-awareness.

Key 9:   Decide on an action plan for positive change.

Key 10: Train your mind to focus only on the positive.

Key 11: Ensure your worldview, core values and guiding principles affirm life.

Key 12: Seek to find and live your purpose, not what is expected of you, popular or merely within your capabilities.

Part 4

Help is at hand

Organisation	Contact	Resource
Australia		
LifeLine	lifeline.org.au	crisis support chat, on line, on phone or email
Kids HelpLine [ages 5 - 25]	kidshelpline.com.au	
Japan		
Tell	telljp.com	support chat, on line, on phone or email
Republic of Ireland		
Samaritans	samaritans.org	hotline, face to face
Russia		
Samaritans - Cherepovets	suicide.org	Hotline, Youth Crisis Line.
United Kingdom		
SANE	sane.org.uk	Chatline
Papyrus Prevention of young suicide	papyrus-uk.org	Telephone chat line
CALM Campain Against Living Miserably	www.thecalmzone.net	Chatline, Web chat

Grassroots Suicide Prevention	prevent-suicide.org.uk	
Anxiety UK	anxietyuk.org.uk	chat line, text line, therapies
Maytree Sanctuary	maytree.org.uk/	Suicide respite centre, counselling
BHCT Beachy Head Chaplaincy Team	bhct.org.uk	Crisis intervention, search and rescue.

United States of America

National Suicide Prevention Lifeline	suicidepreventionlifeline. org	Phone chatline
Lifeline Crisis Chat	crisischat.org	Phone chatline
The Jason Foundation	jasonfoundation.com	Chatline, curriculum studies, 'A Friend Asks' app
Your Life Your Voice	yourlifeyourvoice.org	Chat line, email, text, youtube channel
The Hopeline	thehopeline.com	1 on 1 hopeline chat 24/7.

Final Thoughts

As long as you're alive, change is inevitable. Positive change requires effort, but effort need not be overwhelming. You can pace yourself - step by step.

You may need a helping hand. Help is at hand - you just have to know where to look. Why rush to the point of no return. Why not give yourself as much time as you need to find some answers.

Please note that all the above resources and support services are available as of the time of this book's publication. In the event that one is no longer functioning, please try another.

There is always ...

A Way Out!

Afterword

Those of you who may feel yourselves teetering on the edge of life - a life you deem not worth living – will find reassurance in the motto of living one day at a time. After all, our lives are just a succession of days. If you could just get through the day and see this as an achievement in itself, then perhaps you can do it again tomorrow. Our lives are to be lived in manageable proportions, not in the frustrating attempt to see way up ahead. The spectre of an uncertain future would surely make cowards of us all. Even the most optimistic and courageous amongst us would find this daunting.

Just because you have been wrestling with a problem for some time, doesn't mean you will always wrestle with it until the day you die. Resist your depressive mind's tendency to retreat into yourself and replay the same old messages of gloom and doom. One of the reasons we need to hear one another's stories of conquest is to demonstrate the human potential to overcome challenges and problems.

But know this - ultimately we are all different, and what works for one person, may not work for you. But you too will find your door to victory if you keep searching. As Jesus promised his disciples -*"Ask and it will be given unto you, Seek and you will find, knock and the door will be opened."*[ASK][1]

This book has posed many questions just as life asks many questions of each one of us. Some of the answers don't come easily, and so we need all the time we can get to find the answers. You still have a lot of living to do, and those answers will be worth the wait.

---

1   Matthew 7:7.

Also by the Author

Leaving Normal

This book charts one mother's story so far in her efforts to help her son overcome his medical condition, how she coped with her son's difficult diagnosis and faced the never-ending challenges of his living and learning in residential schools. On the way, she learned to embrace her son and his condition as a blessing, and came to terms with 'leaving normal'. It will appeal to those who care for others in a career, personal or voluntary capacity, or who through disability, struggle to fit into society's stereotype of what 'normal' means.

ISBN 978-1-90797-134-1

Culture Detox

Just as the health and diet industries are promoting detox programmes and diets to improve physical health and well-being, there is also a dire need in our present culture to safeguard our spiritual health.

This book is a culture warrior's perspective on the spiritual dangers of our times. It highlights various worldly contaminants which have infiltrated the modern mind such as the relentless urge to acquire and achieve, the celebrity bandwagon, the widespread use of sex to sell products and seduce, the harmful effects of careless words, and the mass preoccupation with the 'self'. The final chapter presents a spiritual detox programme to help pursue a pure life in these challenging times - "Do not be conformed to this world, but be transformed by the renewing of your mind." [Romans 12:2]

ISBN 978-1-90797-100-6

Captive Daughters

If you've ever questioned your role as a woman in modern society or questioned the stereotypes currently in vogue, then this book is for you. Many women are still captive to:
Choosing inappropriate female role models, usually from the glossy industries of entertainment and fashion where style is valued over substance.
Romantic delusions spun by the Hollywood industry where the focus is on 'boy meets girl' then they live happily ever after with no real understanding of what it takes to stay married.
Trying frenetically to juggle the myriad roles they undertake while still finding time to nurture their

own souls and maintain physical health and well-being.

This book invites you to reflect on current trends, re-examine their validity, then finally break free of their constraining influences.

ISBN 978-1-90797-103-7

Time For Me

A perpetual, devotional calendar designed specifically with the carer in mind. Having been a carer to her autistic son for many years, Carla has a particular insight into the needs of the carer, and can empathise with the tendency to 'burn out' whilst caring for a loved one. To be effective, it is essential to allow time for oneself.

Since carers don't have much time - there's a thought for the day and importantly a suggestion about how to make 'Time For Me'.

ISBN 978-1-85345-428-8

*Available
in Europe from amazon.co.uk
USA, Canada and Worldwide from amazon.com
or the publisher's website jesusjoypublishing.
co.uk*

.